M000233449

Geeky

&

Godly

Science Fiction, Fantasy, & Faith

By Luke Italiano

Illustrated by Ian Samson

Edited by Jennifer Italiano

Geeky & Godly: Science Fiction, Fantasy, & Faith

Text © 2020 Luke Italiano
Illustrations © 2020 Ian Samson

Lofty Publishing

Lofty Publishing, LLC
Norristown, PA 19403
LoftyPublishing.net
GeekyAndGodly.com

FIRST EDITION
April 23, 2021

ISBN: 978-1-77115-485-7 (Color)
ISBN:978-1-77115-486-4 (ePUB)
ISBN:978-1-77115-487-1 (B&W)
ISBN:978-1-77115-488-8 (Hardcover)

For Madelyn

on her Confirmation

Table of Contents

Introduction

Why Epic Tales Matter

Introduction: Why Epic Tales Matter

How the Story Ended

Dragons blotted out the face of the sun. Its light came filtered through the membranous wings of countless enemies. They hovered, staring down with malevolent eyes.

In the barren valley below them, a lone warrior stood knee-deep in a stream, blood covering half his face. He held his blade high. "You wanted my kingdom!" he shouted. "But I give myself in trade. Take me. Take the prince, and leave my kingdom alone!"

The sound of thousands of wings answered him until a dark form descended from the sky. "Prince Charin, come forth!" Zegraun's black scales glittered in the flickering light. His massive form settled onto the valley floor. "Leave your sword behind you."

And so the Prince of the Summerlands thrust Unity, his blade, into the soft ground and made his way unarmed.

The downdraft from the dragon host pushed and prodded him. With every step, the air grew warmer and warmer. Finally, he stood before Zegraun. "I offer my life in exchange for my kingdom. Take my life, and leave the Summerlands, never to return."

"You are in my power, prince. Know this and despair: Now that I have taken you, your kingdom will be mine." The Dragon King exhaled, and fire gushed from his maw, molten stone and flame and heat enough to destroy the strongest of walls.

Charin died.

But he had fooled them all. He had known what would happen. He had taken the Tear of Ice and swallowed it.

And so even as the flames consumed his flesh, the Tear exploded. A wave of clear blue power swept out, swallowing up Zegraun and his generals and the entire dragon host. The King's flames failed. The generals plummeted from the sky. Ice formed on every scale and every wing.

Dragons rained from the heavens. In fives and tens and twenties and countless hosts they plunged to the earth, defeated by the death of the prince.

Thus, by his death, Charin freed the Summerlands. Never again would the dragon host threaten them.

But there are some who say something different. They say that when the Tear of Ice exploded, it healed Prince Charin. They say that he lives still. That he was not merely a prince of this world, but of some greater Kingdom.

Some say he will return to bring his people home from this place merely called the Summerlands to the True Summerlands where winter never comes.

But perhaps that is a story for another time.

God Tells Stories

When God wanted to tell us about himself, he told a story. He didn't make up some epic tale to try and sell books or get people to watch his great show. He told us the true tale of how things came to be the way they are.

God's a storyteller.

He spoke about a world stunning in its beauty. He painted a sky that sang in sunlight and mountains that shouted majesty. He told about two people literally made for each other.

And then God told us what happened next: Those first two people chose to reject the one who made all creation for their enjoyment. They thought they could do better. And when they walked away from their Creator, all creation cried out in pain and sorrow.

And thus, our world was born.

A world that though it still reflected some of that original beauty, was broken beyond any of our abilities to repair. Now the sky sang fury. Now the mountains shouted fear. Now people made for each other would cause each other grief. Now every single person would have to say goodbye. There was no forever.

There was a price to pay for our rebellion: death.

There was a price to pay for our rebellion: death. Once we became rebels (and that's what we are by nature), we could not come into God's presence. He is a God who punishes those who reject him.

We couldn't fix creation. We couldn't even fix ourselves.

The story plunged to an ending so tragic that we should just give up.

But God wrote a new character into the tragedy: himself. Jesus, the Son of God, chose to walk this earth and bear the burden of our rebellion. All creation held its breath as he was born in a city named Bethlehem. As he grew, he walked this world in perfect harmony with his Father. But just as he was rejected at the beginning of time, now he was rejected again. And as he went to the cross, as he was executed, he bore our punishment. He chose to pay the price for us. He died in our place.

And we got away free.

But that wasn't the end of the story. For three days, creation mourned. And then creation rejoiced.

Its Prince, Jesus, was alive again. Because Jesus had never once rebelled, he didn't have to pay the cost himself. Death could not hold him. On the third day, he walked out of the grave, alive again. And he still lives today.

See, in this book called the Bible, God told the story of what he did for us. Sure, there are rules there. And there are instructions. And there's stunning poetry.

But a lot of it is a story.

God's a storyteller, and the stories he tells are the best stories, because they're true. Every syllable. They're about how he rescued us. How he sacrificed himself for us and now lives again – for us.

God's Not the Only Storyteller

The story God tells in his Word, the Bible, is fascinating... but you've noticed it's not the only story.

What about the story of a boy who lives under the stairs until he finds out he's a wizard?

What about the story of intrepid explorers trekking through the stars in their majestic ship?

What about the story of a young hero from a desert planet wanting to become a guardian of peace like his father before him?

> *But God wrote a new character into the tragedy: himself.*

What about the story of a madman with a blue box?

Oh, there are so many good stories, aren't there? God created humans to reflect his qualities. One of the ways that appears is that we love telling stories, too. And we love hearing stories. If you've made it this far, you already know about at least some of those stories. You probably do more than know about them, though. You love them. Maybe not all of them, but enough to call yourself a bit of a geek.

Maybe a big geek.

That's all right. I'm a geek, too. I don't remember my first comic book; my dad bought them for me further back than I can recall. I still stop by my comic shop every week. I grew up watching *Star Trek* and *Star Wars* and *Doctor Who* and many other science fiction shows. I loved *The Chronicles of Narnia* and *Lord of the Rings* and all those books. I'm not afraid to admit it: I'm a geek!

I'm also one of those people that loves Jesus. After all, he loved me first! That love has led me to be a pastor and share Jesus with anyone I can. You could say I geek out about Jesus at least sometimes.

But it also means that I often evaluate what I take in for entertainment through a distinctly Christian lens.

It's a Matter of Discernment

Is it okay to enjoy geeky pursuits?

Well, no.

And yes.

Some things aren't a matter of right or wrong. Sometimes God allows us to use human judgment to evaluate whether or not something is good for us. I'm not saying there is no such thing as right or wrong; God gave us his Ten Commandments for a reason! But sometimes God isn't explicit about certain things we face in life, and then we need to figure it out.

Here's an encouragement: God doesn't say, "Thou shalt stay away from science fiction." Yes! I can still enjoy my favorite stories!

But he also doesn't say, "Memorize your favorite lines from *The Princess Bride*, for they are useful for training in righteousness." So, no command to enjoy them, either.

Philippians 4:8 gives us this guidance: "Finally brothers and sisters, whatever is true, whatever is honorable, whatever is just, whatever is pure, whatever is lovely, whatever is commendable—if there is any moral excellence and if there is anything praiseworthy—dwell on these things."

So... the things we geek out about, you and me, are they praiseworthy? Well, we sure praise them. I know I tell my family a lot about my favorite episodes or books or issues. But... does that make them worthy of praise? Are they pure? Are they lovely? Are they honorable?

Well, no.

And yes.

Kinda depends, doesn't it?

Again, it's not a matter of right or wrong. It's a matter of discernment. It means we need to use our human reason to evaluate our geeky pursuits in the light of God's Word.

Doomed to a World You Didn't Create

So, how do we determine if a particular piece of geekery, a certain book or show, is good for us?

Something you want to ask: Are you longing for a world God didn't create?

> *Sure, Aslan was written to be a picture of Jesus, but isn't the reality better than any picture?*

This question will be the biggest obstacle for you. Some of the worlds in fiction are so attractive they can suck you in. And if you lose track of what is real, you've gone too far.

I remember loving *The Chronicles of Narnia* when I was younger. There was something magical about holding those books more than any other book. And then at night, I stopped praying to Jesus and started praying to Aslan.

Was I wrong?

Yeah, I was going too far.

Sure, Aslan was written to be a picture of Jesus, but isn't the reality better than any picture?

But I had turned a good story that really does point to Jesus into an idol. I preferred that story to the real one.

Ask: Does this help draw me closer to Jesus, to appreciate the brokenness of this world while rejoicing in his forgiveness? Or does it take me further away from him?

Because no matter how good it seems, if it takes you from Jesus, it is no longer good.

That doesn't mean your favorite geekable fiction is bad. It means, again, you need to use discernment.

> *A trope is a commonly used plot device.*

What's in a Trope?

So, there's a lot of things to geek out over. I could write out a book about *Lord of the Rings* or *Star Trek* or any of my favorite geeky pursuits, but I think getting so specific won't help as much. Instead, I'm going to talk about common tropes used in science fiction and fantasy.

> *In short, we'll be looking for reflections of the Greatest Story, the story God told in the Bible, in the stories we love so much.*

A trope is a commonly used plot device. For instance, many science fiction shows need to find fast ways to get around. Maybe they use a portal or a teleporter or hyper-light-superspeed. Each of those is a different trope. A trope might be a type of character, like a chosen one or a nerdy sidekick, or it could be a plot device, like the destruction of a sanctuary or super-fast aging.

We're going to attempt to use discernment to talk about some common tropes.

We'll look to see what problem this trope is attempting to resolve. Then we'll ask what solution it proposes. By looking for the problem and the solution, we'll find out a lot about why these tropes exist and what we can learn from them.

In short, we'll be looking for reflections of the Greatest Story, the story God told in the Bible, in the stories we love so much. We're going to find a lot of reflections... and a lot of darkness that detracts from God's story.

That's probably enough introduction, isn't it? About time we start digging in?

All right. Let's do this.

Trope One

Outer Space

"WE SHOULD HAVE TURNED LEFT AT ANTARES."

Trope 1: Outer Space

Battle for the Stars

Look, space travel is dangerous. All the time. You gotta deal with micro asteroids and explosive decompression, and let's not forget just plain old freezing. So yeah, death is always a distinct possibility. I'm told it's usually worth it, though. You get to see nebulae and comets and novas.

Right now all I was seeing was DeCart's fist.

Did you know that a fist hurts your face just as much in space as it does on Earth? Yeah. I learned that the hard way.

And it started during liftoff, too. My first chance to leave this stupid ball of dirt and see the stars. To finally travel. And DeCart's trying to kill me.

I fell back and scrambled away. The brute loomed over me; his fists clenched. "You thought you could steal it from me, huh? This is my chance to shine! Not yours, punk!"

"DeCart, look, they found out you cheated. You can't cheat in space! Things try to kill you out here!"

He punched the wall in anger. Some sparks flew. We probably needed that for something silly like re-entry later. He growled at me, "Well, buddy, too late. Now I'm on this ship with you, and we're all going to the Colonies."

"Yeah, no. There's not enough food for another mouth. Everything's figured out. You're with us now, but now... someone's gonna starve."

And this big ol' smile lit up his face. "That's right, buddy. I forgot about that. But see, I already have a solution. I'll just kill you like I shoulda done back at the academy." He lunged at me.

I didn't have a chance. He's bigger than me. Stronger. Meaner. Faster.

But I had a space suit, since I was supposed to be here, and he snuck on in jeans and a t-shirt.

Did you know that we decompress the cabin on the way up?

Oops.

His eyes rolled up, and he collapsed as the deck continued to shake. We'd left atmosphere for sure. I hauled myself to my feet and stood over him, huffing and puffing. I'm still not used to fistfights. I could have just left him there. He would have died.

But I figured I shouldn't let my first action off mudball Earth be letting some creep die.

If I was going to save his life, though, I had to get him dressed quick. And something he didn't know since he cheated – I could probably drop him out an airlock, and he'd float back to Earth fairly safe, as long as I got him out quick.

You ever try to stuff an unconscious lout into a space suit? It's kind of like stuffing a giant squid into a tin can. You can make it work, but it's probably not comfortable for the squid.

I didn't mind that part so much.

I popped open the airlock, and DeCart flew right out and down. Got him out just in time; he should be safe, and now no one would starve.

Whoa.

Look at that. The arc of the earth. You see it in pictures, but it's not the same. And now... I'm going out there. Finally. Leaving everything behind.

I get to go out to the Colonies. And after that?

Maybe even farther.

A Spacey Trope

Stories happen in places, and for many stories, the place is space. Somewhere... out there. Often it happens in the future, but it could happen right now or in the past, too. But it's off our planet's surface, somewhere in the black.

Often enough, spaceships of some kind are involved (though not necessarily). There might be an alien world to explore or interact with. There might be aliens (but we'll talk about them later). The main characters can interact with all sorts of spacey things like supernovas and comets and rifts. Space stations might be visited.

But space is the place.

To Boldly Go

Why do so many stories go to outer space? There's a lot of reasons, aren't there? If we're going to use discernment about stories in space, we need to figure out why we like being someplace that isn't here. What problem is the story attempting to solve, and what solution does it suggest?

We all have this desire to explore.

Sometimes, the setting of outer space isn't about any problem other than, "I want to see what's out there." Humans often have this drive to explore, and the setting of outer space helps us achieve that exploration.

And that drive to explore is something God put into us. Genesis 1:28 says, "God blessed them, and God said to them, 'Be fruitful, multiply, fill the earth, and subdue it. Rule the fish of the sea, the birds of the sky, and every creature that crawls on the earth.' "

Did you catch that? Fill the earth. Subdue it. We could fill the earth and subdue it right where we are, but there's so much *more* out there. Go fill it all up. Go see what's out there.

Now, God didn't tell us to abuse what we would discover. While we won't be talking about environmentalism in this book, we do want to note that God did give us this world to take care of. He didn't tell us to crush what we found or destroy it. Just... go and see.

We all have this desire to explore. Sometimes it shows up as actually physically going into the wilderness. Sometimes it shows up as exploring how the world works. Sometimes it shows up as the need to read stories about people that go out there. Psalms 8, 19, and 139 all marvel at the wonders of creation and the God who put all that there. We are hardwired to appreciate and see what else God put into creation.

So, there's this problem: We have a drive to see what's out there.

The solution: Go see what's out there! Let's explore the universe! Out into space!

As far as problems and solutions go, these are pretty solid. We *do* have that drive! We *can* explore! Look with wonder at this universe God's created!

Of course, often enough in these stories we're not just going into outer space to explore. Sometimes there's an ulterior motive...

It's Out There... Somewhere

Sometimes in stories that take place in outer space, we're not just out there to explore. There's some problem that needs solving. Whatever this problem is, there's no solution on Earth. But maybe, just maybe, we can find the answer out among the stars.

> *Every human knows that there is something wrong with this world.*

Maybe it's overpopulation. We need a new place to live.

Maybe we've run out of natural resources. We need to find a new source of water or food.

Maybe we've run out of energy. We need some new means to power our civilization.

There's a lot of maybes here. But what binds them all is this nagging suspicion that we can't find what we need on this planet.

Something is lacking. Hopefully, the answer is out there.

And as far as such stories go, they can usually find the answer out there, can't they? Space stations and colonies alleviate overpopulation. Fresh fields grow all sorts of new foods. Look at all those innovative sources of power!

But there's this underlying theme: Earth isn't good enough to solve the problems we have.

That's actually... kind of a neat realization for someone to have. It's a reflection, just a glimmer, of a much deeper truth: We are broken, and if something is going to fix us, that solution isn't going to be from here. I'm talking about something much bigger and darker than limited natural resources or overpopulation, though.

Every human knows that there is something *wrong* with this world. We can *feel* it. We say things like, "It's not supposed to be that way," or "That's not fair." We have this imperative that says some things are right and some things are wrong. We will disagree, sometimes in very violent ways, about what things are right or wrong, but very few people will say there's no such thing as right or wrong – not when you get down to it. And if they say there's no such thing as right or wrong, try stealing their lunch. See if they still think there's no such thing as right or wrong.

We get that there's something wrong. And many people have tried fixing it. They have tried with positive thinking or rules or just starting over. But it always falls apart. If we could fix it, we would have already.

There's some wisdom in that, actually!

But the problem is... we're not going to find the solution *out there* either. And we're not going to find the solution in anything we do.

Because the thing that's wrong... is us.

The Bible calls it sin. See, God set up this universe to work a certain way, and then... we disagreed with him. The problem is, God was right, and we were wrong. And we continue to be wrong. When we think or say or do something wrong, something that doesn't agree with God, we sin.

God says, "Don't steal."

We answer, "Well, yeah. Don't steal. Except for this thing right here, because really, that's not *really* stealing."

God says, "Don't deceive."

> *The solution is out there. It's not from us.*

We answer, "Obviously! No one should deceive someone else. Unless they've got a good reason. Or it's me just trying to avoid getting in trouble. A little white lie doesn't count."

We can't fix us, whether we're using methods we uncover here on Earth or something out beyond Proxima VII.

But the solution did come from somewhere outside this planet. John 3:16 says, "For God loved the world in this way: He gave his one and only Son, so that everyone who believes in him will not perish but have eternal life." God himself had the solution to us turning away from him.

The solution was himself.

God sent us Jesus. Not as an example to show us how to fix ourselves. Not as a teacher to try and tame us.

He sent Jesus as a substitute.

Instead of us having to pay up for all the times we thought we knew better than God and ended up screwing up God's creation, Jesus paid for us on the cross.

So, when all these stories say that the solution is out there, they've got a little inkling of something very true: The solution is out there. It's not from us. But we don't have to go looking for it. He found us.

Now you need to use your discernment: Does the story you're experiencing send the message that humanity can overcome every problem as long as we go out there and find it? Honestly, that's not a great message. Be aware of it. God has given us the ability to overcome a lot of obstacles. We can cure some diseases. We can find new sources of energy.

But we can't fix us.

And if the story teaches that we can fix us... it's sending a false message. When that's the message, make sure you notice it and say, "Well, this story might be a fun story, but the message is wrong."

Sometimes you can use your love of geeky things to talk to others about Jesus.

But look out for those little reflections of Jesus. Look for those little inklings that say, "We have to find the solution outside of ourselves." And when you see them, smile to yourself. Whether or not the story knows it, it's found something true.

Sometimes You Just Gotta Get Out to Space...

And sometimes a story takes place in outer space... just because that's where the story happens. It doesn't have to do with exploration, and it's not that some problem can't be solved on Earth. Sometimes the writer just said, "I have this cool idea, *and it's gonna happen on a spaceship!*"

And there's nothing wrong with that! Space is a pretty cool place to be.

The question for you in your discernment is this:

Why is the story in space?

Is it a cool place to be? Is it exploring wonders? Is it finding a solution to another problem?

Using Space to Share Jesus

Sometimes you can use your love of geeky things to talk to others about Jesus. Here's a suggestion on how to use your love of stories that take place in outer space to serve as a bridge to talk to others about Jesus. Imagine yourself saying:

"Isn't it cool how people leave Earth to find solutions? I mean, look!" (And then talk about a favorite story where that happens.) "But there's a problem... I mean, look, there's a problem here, right? Earth isn't the way it's supposed to be. But have you noticed we keep on failing to fix it?

"Maybe that's because the problem is bigger than us. Or maybe... we're the problem. We can't fix us.

"But I know someone who can. Someone who came from outside to fix us. And we don't have to go out into outer space to find him. Let me tell you about Jesus..."

Are You Pondering What I'm Pondering?

The next time you experience a story set in space, ask a few questions:

- ✓ What made it necessary to set this story in space?
- ✓ Is this a problem that the Bible agrees is a problem?
- ✓ What solution does this story propose to the problem?
- ✓ Does this solution show a reflection of the knowledge of God, or does it push against it?

The next time you enjoy a story set in space, ask a few questions:

- ✓ Why am I enjoying this story set in space? Do I have a drive to explore God's creation?
- ✓ Do I think that I might be able to find the solutions to my biggest problems somewhere else? Or am I content to say that Jesus is the solution to my biggest problem: sin?
- ✓ Am I just enjoying a story that's somewhere out there?

Meditations on Outer Space

Wonders Near and Far

You ever watch the night sky and go, "Wow"? There's a reason that for millennia people have looked up at the stars and wondered what's out there. And now with the best telescopes, we have some beautiful pictures of nebulae and novas and neutron stars... It is amazing. It doesn't matter what you believe; when you stand in the face of such wonder you have to say, "Wow."

Could you count up the wonders of creation? Even if you limit it to things off this planet, there's so much out there. Just try: The wonders of gravity and dark matter and comets and the rings around Saturn and...

Well, we could keep going.

Psalm 40:5 agrees. It says, "LORD my God, you have done many things – your wondrous works..." There's this gasp at just how many wonders God has put out there for us to discover.

But the verse continues: "LORD my God, you have done many things – your wondrous works and your plans for us."

It's not just what God did out there that takes the breath away. It's what God did here, too. Psalm 40:1 – the first verse of that Psalm we just quoted – says, "I waited patiently for the LORD, and he turned to me and heard my cry for help."

> The God who created the stars cared enough about you to become human.

Think about how big God is. Think about those wonders he created out in space. In Genesis 1, when God creates them, they're almost an afterthought. "Oh, yeah. And God created stars, too." That's how powerful God is. That's how big he is.

And he listens to *you*. He's that big, and he still cares enough about you that when you cry out to him, he turns his whole attention to you, to listen to you, and to do what is best for you.

The God who created the stars cared enough about you to become human. Can you imagine going from lighting stars to not being able to lift your own head? And yet he cared enough for you to do that. He cared enough to go from crafting stellar clouds to walking this dusty planet. He cared enough to step away from designing gravity itself to instead be beaten and killed for you.

This is wonder.

When you look at the stars, yes, celebrate that God would create such amazing parts of his world for us to marvel at. But also remember that the God who's so big and powerful cared enough about you to hear your cry for help... and answer.

Prayer: Father, you made the stars, and you crafted the night sky. Yet you cared enough to step down to our dusty planet and make it your home. You cared enough about me, so small, that you died for me. Thank you. Help me look with wonder on your creation and how you saved me. Amen.

It's Not Up to You.

All that weight lands on Jesus.

I mentioned before that the solution to the brokenness of this world must come from outside of us. That we can't fix our problems.

Did that offend you at all?

It's not the usual message of science fiction or fantasy, is it? "You have to believe in yourself!" is a common refrain. And it feels plenty good to hear that. "You can do it!"

But there's a big problem with that: If you can do it, if you have to believe in yourself... that means it's all up to you. It means that if you fail, it's your fault. It's your responsibility to fix everything.

That is a *huge* weight. It's more than I can bear! You?

But if the solution to our brokenness and this broken world comes from outside us... then it's not our responsibility to fix it. God had to come in and offer the solution. In fact, he said he'd even bear the weight: Isaiah 9:6 says, "For a child will be born for us, a son will be given to us, and the government will be on his shoulders." See that? The weight of the government of the world – the weight of ruling the world and fixing its problems – it's not on us. All that weight lands on Jesus.

Pressure's off.

1 John 4:9 says, "God's love was revealed among us in this way: God sent his one and only Son into the world so that we might live through him." He came from outside the world... so that we might live.

Maybe you're thinking, "Well, if the pressure's off, now I can just sit and read all day. It's God's job to fix the world. I can just enjoy my stories!"

Wait a second. He came... so that we might live. Not so that we could turn our backs on the world. It's so we know that we can rely on him. He has rescued us. The deed is done.

But now we get to live and show love to those around us. Jesus rescued them, too. And just as Jesus served them, now we get to serve. Not to fix the world; we can't do that. But to show love to those around us, just like Jesus showed love to us.

Prayer: Sometimes I think it's up to me to fix the world. Forgive me, Jesus. Only you can fix the world. You have come to me in my brokenness and loved me. Thank you. Help me stay away from thinking it's up to me and stay away from apathy. Instead, let me trust you even as you point me to ways to serve here. Amen.

Just Imagine...

What lies beyond where any human has seen? What awaits us in the darkness?

Is it terrifying? Are there creatures made to withstand the rigors of space that could eat planets whole?

Is it beautiful? Is it so stunning that we would simply sit and stare until we wasted away to nothing?

Is it nothing? Is it just more of the same the farther out you go?

Any which way, it boggles the imagination, doesn't it? It's so much fun to think about what's out there, and it's my guess you love stories that wonder what might lie beyond.

Have you thanked God for the gift of imagination? Have you considered what a blessing imagination is? It lies at the root of anything new – not just new stories, but new inventions, new homes, new relationships! God knew what he was doing when he put this part of us into motion. I, for one, am grateful!

God knows what you've imagined, even if you've never told anyone.

That doesn't mean that all imagination is good, of course. People use imagination to think up new ways to hurt one another (or repeat old ways with new creative twists). People use imagination to come up with new ways to claim that God has nothing to do with them.

Just like any other blessing, though God intended it for good, to enrich our lives and point back to his goodness to us, we tend to twist imagination. Have you ever used your imagination to picture something sinful and then reveled in that sin?

Yes, God reads the heart. He knows what you've imagined, even if you've never told anyone.

But what God knows... he has forgiven. Colossians 2:13 says, "And when you were dead in trespasses... he made you alive with [Jesus] and forgave us all our trespasses."

All of them. Even the ones of our imagination.

So now... yeah, thank God for your imagination. Praise him by using your imagination to think of God's wonders! Philippians 4:8 says, "Finally brothers and sisters, whatever is true, whatever is honorable, whatever is just, whatever is pure, whatever is lovely, whatever is commendable – if there is any moral excellence and if there is anything praiseworthy – dwell on these things." Use your imagination, yes! But use it to think of things that are honorable and good.

Prayer: Thank you, Jesus, for my imagination. Forgive me for the many times I've used my imagination to think about things that are impure or hurtful. Help me to use it in ways that will bring you glory. In your name, Amen.

Trope Two

Aliens

"OH, I ONLY NEED 2 1/2 HUMANS. PUT THE
REST BACK IN THE FRIDGE."

Trope 2: Aliens

The Rocks Send Greetings

"What is it?" Captain Devereaux squinted at the screen.

Lieutenant Cannon checked her monitors again. "It's just an asteroid, sir. But it's matched our speed and heading, directly in front of us, about five kilometers out."

"No propulsion?"

"Sir, it's a chunk of rock."

Devereaux tilted his head. "Change course, ten degrees up."

"Ten degrees up, aye." Cannon worked her magic, and the hum of the engines altered slightly.

The rock matched them again.

"Sir," Cannon breathed, watching her sensors. "The asteroid isn't alone." She put her readings up on the screen. Three more red dots appeared, flanking them port, starboard, and below. "Several more asteroids matching course and speed. Hemming us in." As she spoke, more flickering dots appeared.

"Will our torpedoes be able to knock them out of the way?"

"Well, sure. If they're normal asteroids. But –" Cannon waved at the screen, flabbergasted.

Devereaux sat in his chair, considering the screen. He hummed to himself – a tune from old earth. *Bolero.* That was probably a bad sign. "All stop."

"All stop, aye." Cannon pushed the commands through her panels.

The rocks all matched them.

And then they floated closer. Four kilometers. Three. Two. And then they stopped. Now there were thirty-seven of them, fairly evenly spaced in a sphere around the ship.

And then they shifted again. Formed a new pattern.

The captain blinked. "Is that what I think it is?"

"Yes, sir," Cannon answered.

The rocks had shifted to form two English letters: "Hi."

"Well, at least they're friendly rocks," Devereaux mused. "How do you think we say 'hi' back?"

The Trope is Out There

There are aliens! There's life out there, and they ain't from here! Maybe they're little green men from Mars. Maybe they're an honorable race seeking to conquer others. Maybe they're peaceful people who reveal how savage humans really are. Maybe they're bacteria or ride around in three-legged vehicles or have two hearts in their chests. Maybe they look just like us.

They can show up in fantasy stories, too – but we're going to be focusing mostly on science fiction for this one. Believe it or not, we'll discuss orcs in a later trope, so if you're looking for that, just hold on for that chapter!

They come in many shapes and many sizes, but in this trope, we see that there's life out there... and it's alien.

We Are Not Alone

Have you ever considered why so many science fiction and fantasy stories assume that there's other life out there?

In shows like *Star Wars* or *Star Trek* or *Doctor Who* or just about any space opera, space seems crowded with just how many planets developed life. A large part of such shows digs into other cultures and biologies and how everyone interacts with each other.

If we are alone... does that make us freaks?

Why do you think so many stories make that choice?

For most, I would guess it's simply because someone is looking to tell an engaging story, and having aliens is one way to achieve that goal.

But *why* is it so engaging?

Consider the alternative: What if we're alone in the universe? What if humans are all there is for intelligent species? What would that mean?

If we are alone... does that make us freaks? Does that make humans the strangest thing this universe has ever come up with? Should we even feel ashamed of our very existence, since no other planets deemed fit to produce anything remotely similar to us?

Or maybe the opposite is true. Maybe we're alone because we're special.

If you have a universe populated with all sorts of aliens, you don't have to wonder if we're special or if we're freaks. We're just one more species out there scooting among the stars. Instead of pondering what makes us special, we get to just learn about all the other weirdos out there.

But what if... let's look at that second option again. What if we're special?

That's a real scary thought. If we're special, we probably have some special purpose. Maybe we have a special responsibility. Maybe we're held to a special standard.

What if *you're* special? Can you bear that burden? What if it's actually true that, as *VeggieTales* says, "God made you special, and he loves you very much"?

If what makes you special depends on you, you can lose it at any time.

John 1:14 says, "The Word became flesh and dwelt among us." God became human. He didn't become a Klingon or a Time Lord. He didn't even become a dolphin or a hamster. He became our brother, a man named Jesus. That makes us special: God chose to become one of us.

And the reason he became one of us? Galatians 4:4-5 says, "When the time came to completion, God sent his Son, born of a woman, born under the law, to redeem those under the law, so that we might receive adoption as sons." God became one of us, having to keep all the same laws we do, and he did it to redeem us.

"Redeem" is a word we don't use a whole lot. It means "buy back." He bought us back from death and our own sin. And the price he paid was his own blood on the cross. We belong to him now. Sin and death hold no claim on us.

You see, what makes us special isn't whether we're alone in the universe... what makes us special is that God redeemed us. What makes us special isn't what we do, but what God did for us to make us his own.

This might sound horrible. It might sound like some alien conqueror saying, "Yes, human, you are so special that I bought you from Yorblax the Gregarious to use you for seasoning on my salad!" Because, after all, if what makes us special is God redeeming us, well, that doesn't exactly make me feel great about myself. Belonging to someone else doesn't necessarily make us feel good about ourselves – we got bought, for crying out loud!

But it's amazing. If what makes you special is up to you, you can lose it at any time. If your musical ability makes you special, what happens when you don't have time to practice? If your height makes you special, what happens when someone else is taller than you? If having a boyfriend or girlfriend makes you special, what happens when you break up? If what makes you special depends on you, you can lose it at any time.

But if what makes you special depends on God... that special-ness can't be lost.

And what makes you special is something very cool indeed: God loves you. The God who created the universe thought you were so important that he had to pay any price to make you his own. He paid to adopt you into his family. He wants you to belong with him.

So, what does all this have to do with aliens?

When you're experiencing a story that has lots of aliens, you can ask, "Why are there all these aliens here?" Is it because the person telling the story doesn't think humans are special? We're just one more species among countless?

If that's their reason, I hope you know better now!

The Universe is Terrifying

Sometimes we encounter aliens in stories not because humanity isn't special. Sometimes the storyteller believes something else: We have a reason to fear. The universe doesn't care about us. We are a cosmic blip on the radar, and we will be destroyed.

You can find this kind of reasoning in *Alien* or H. P. Lovecraft's Cthulhu mythos (or the many stories that follow that philosophy, including the original *Conan* stories). When the alien is huge and doesn't care about humans, when the outsider can wipe us out without thinking too hard, it is often symptomatic of this philosophy.

These stories often result in one of two messages:

First, the universe doesn't care about us. Therefore, rage against death itself. Fight back. You're not special according to the universe; it's up to you to stand your ground and make sure our species survives.

This sounds really noble at first blush. I gotta tell you, when I watch movies like *Aliens* where Ripley stands her ground against the Xenomorphs, I get really into it. And when she wins against all odds? That makes for a great story.

> *You can't fight back – on your own. You do not have that strength.*

And there's some truth here, isn't there? There are parts of the universe that not only aren't friendly to you; there are powers in this universe that want to destroy you.

Demons want you dead. They want to tear you away from Jesus and will do whatever it takes to achieve their goal. They're bigger than you. More powerful than you. You can't fight back. No matter how much you try to act like Ripley, all heroic and strong, your strength is not enough. Ephesians 6:12-13 says, "For our struggle is not against flesh and blood, but against the rulers, against the authorities, against the cosmic powers of this darkness, against evil, spiritual forces in the heavens. For this reason, take up the full armor of God, so that you may be able to resist in the evil day, and having prepared everything, to take your stand."

Wait a second! That Bible verse says to take your stand! Didn't I just say you couldn't fight back?

I did.

But put on God's armor.

You can't fight back – on your own. You do not have that strength.

But put on God's armor. You can read more about that in Ephesians 6, picking up right after those last verses. It's worth a look. And there you'll see: What God provides protects you. The same Jesus that was more powerful than demons when he walked this earth is still more powerful than any demon that can attack you.

The strength isn't in you. It's in him.

And the good news of that: When you're too weak to fight back, Jesus himself protects you.

But if you Can't Fight Back...

If the story you're experiencing deals with a big, uncaring universe, it may have the message: Fight back! The second message you might see could be phrased this way: The universe is big and uncaring, so just give up. There is no meaning. Resign yourself to this fact.

But... you just read in that Ephesians passage: "Take your stand!" You aren't called to give up. As someone who knows Jesus, you are called to stand against the darkness!

The problem proposed in all these stories boils down to: The universe doesn't care.

Both solutions – "Fight back" and "Give up" – boil down to the same message: It's up to you to deal with it.

In some of these tropes, we'll see that the observed problem is right on, but the solution doesn't measure up. This time around though, we see that the problem is actually wrong!

While the *universe* might not care about us, since the universe is not a thinking being, *God*, who created the universe, does care about us. Romans 5:8 says, "But God proves his own love for us in that while we were still sinners, Christ died for us."

You don't die for someone you don't care about.

And if God's on our side... who could stand against us? Demons or aliens or the darkness of space?

Nothing.

Don't fear. Put on the armor God himself provides. Stand in the knowledge that God not only cares about you; he went out to find you and willingly paid to make you his own again.

Maybe it's Not about the Aliens...

The reasons for having aliens in a story can be many.

Sometimes the aliens are there to show we aren't special. Sometimes the aliens are there to say the universe doesn't care about us.

And sometimes the aliens exist in a story to reveal something about us.

Is the story exploring xenophobia (fear of strangers/people different from us)? Does it show our reaction to alien visitors to make us examine our reaction to humans that just happen to be different?

Is the story showing us something silly about how our government works by casting it in a different light? (Jonathon Swift did this brilliantly in *Gulliver's Travels*.)

Is the story helping us grasp the need to show compassion to one another by introducing an alien race that doesn't show compassion?

In all these cases, the story isn't about the aliens. It's about us. The story reveals something about humanity by making us examine particular human qualities in an alien setting.

And in those cases... it's not about the aliens. Try to see what message the story is sending. What assumptions does it make? What's the problem? What's the proposed solution?

In the end, using aliens in a story doesn't mark a story as bad for Christians to take in. We do want to be smart, though. Use your discernment. Why did the storyteller choose to use aliens? Are those aliens there to teach us something? Are they just there so we have an enemy to fight in the story? (In which case, head on down to the chapter on orcs!) Is there something more going on?

The reasons for having aliens in a story can be many; we just addressed a few here. But hopefully it gave you a good start so you can use your discernment the next time visitors from another planet pop up in your stories.

Using Aliens to Share Jesus

So, I spent a lot of time talking about why stories might include aliens, but are there aliens out there? Are there other species populating other planets?

Simply put: The Bible doesn't answer that question.

The Bible *does* call humans the crown of creation, the part of creation created "in God's image" (Check out Genesis 1 for more on that). So yes, I will maintain that even should there be aliens out there, humans are a special part of creation. Even if there are aliens out there, God became one of us, became human, to redeem us. That marks us as special.

Are there other species populating other planets?

Personally, I think that there is more life out there, but none of it sentient life. But like I said: I think. That's my opinion, and merely my opinion. You're welcome to disagree with it!

However, because the Bible doesn't say whether or not there is life out there, we should be careful when we get into discussions with others. We don't have to argue one way or another *as Christians.* You can share your opinion, but don't be dogmatic about it!

But if you happen to be talking with someone about whether or not there are aliens, you can say you're confident that we aren't alone in the universe. You can even say that someone far more advanced than us humans has visited the earth!

In fact, God himself lived among us. Yeah, he's not an alien the way you'd think. Most aliens would kinda stand out, right? But the Bible says that he was fully human. What kind of aliens *become* humans, unless they're going undercover? But Jesus? Instead of going undercover to be sneaky, he does it to be our substitute.

That's pretty cool, isn't it?

You can even say that someone far more advanced than us humans has visited the earth!

Are You Pondering What I'm Pondering?

The next time you experience a story that uses aliens from outer space, ask some questions:

- ✓ Why did the storyteller choose to use aliens in this story?

- ✓ Do the aliens prove that humans are not special – that we are just one among many in the universe?

- ✓ Do the aliens prove that the universe is an uncaring place?

- ✓ Are the aliens used to reveal something about humanity? If so, what do they reveal?

- ✓ Does the use of aliens reveal any presuppositions on the part of the storyteller? If so, what are they, and do they match biblical presuppositions?

The next time you enjoy a story with aliens, ask some questions:

- ✓ What about this story appeals to me? Am I being drawn to a story that teaches that humans aren't special, and if so, what am I taking in?

- ✓ Do I enjoy the horror of thinking that there are creatures that can destroy me so quickly? If so, how can I be reminded that though there are demons that can easily wipe me out, God is both way more powerful and actually loves me?

- ✓ If I am enjoying exploring alien civilizations, would it be worth my time to explore foreign human civilizations and see how varied our cultures on Earth are?

Meditations on Aliens

Ancient Aliens?

There are some neat designs for aliens. Go ahead and google "imaginative alien designs," and you'll find a plethora of fascinating ideas. They're just so... out there!

But have you ever read some descriptions of aliens from the Bible? Go read Ezekiel 1. I'll wait here. I'm not going to type that whole Bible chapter here. Go ahead and read it from your own Bible or phone.

> *Take a look at what happens when angels show up in the Bible.*

So, those funky angels with four heads and wheels and all that? Those are called "cherubim." Aren't they just weird? That isn't the normal picture of an angel you'll find at your local Hobby Lobby!

Could it be that when people talk about meeting aliens today... they're talking about angels? Maybe they *have* encountered something not human, but it was a spiritual visitor instead of a visitor from another planet!

But take a look at what happens when angels show up in the Bible. Read Luke 1 and 2. Read Matthew 1. Read Luke 24:1-12. Go ahead and use the search function at biblegateway.com or a concordance and look up as many references to angels as you'd like.

When angels show up, they don't just randomly kidnap people or even just scare them. (This is probably why I'm not an angel; I'd love using the abilities of an angel to freak people out!)

When angels show up, they do one of two things: They announce God's Word, or they protect God's people.

When aliens seem to show up, like in *X-Files*, is that what they're doing?

Not so much, huh?

So, if what people are seeing is real and not a hallucination of some kind, what are they seeing? 2 Corinthians 11:14 says, "Satan disguises himself as an angel of light." If Satan can appear as something he's not to drive people away from Jesus, to scare them or to make them chase after something that isn't Jesus, he'll do it. Why not as an alien?

I won't say that every alien appearance that someone jabbers on about is demonic activity. There's a lot of drunkenness and drugs and mental imbalance that can cause people to think they've seen something that wasn't there. But some of it *could* be something real and very sinister.

What do you do about it?

Know that there are scary things out there.

Know that Jesus is more powerful.

He bound demons while here on earth, and he's still here with his people. You are not alone. Jesus bought you with his own blood. He's not about to let some demon masquerading as an alien take you away from him!

Prayer: Jesus, sometimes I enjoy stories about aliens, and I wonder if there are any out there. You created such amazing things – maybe there are aliens! But protect me from any force that tries to get between you and me. You rescued me from my sins and have given me eternal life; I don't need anything else. Amen.

A Deadly Universe

Sometimes the aliens in a story are unbeatable. If humanity survives, it is by mere luck. These are usually very dark stories that frighten us with our helplessness.

There's a kernel of truth in those stories.

Listen to what it says in Psalm 23:4: "Even when I go through the darkest valley [or the valley of the shadow of death], I fear no danger, for you are with me."

Go ahead and read all of Psalm 23. It's well worth your time.

Notice it doesn't say "If I go through the valley of the shadow of death." It doesn't say, "Even when I have some little troubles." It doesn't say, "Sometimes I get really miffed, but I know I'll make it, because nothing could really be that bad." It says "when."

The Bible can be really stunning with how bluntly it talks about darkness. Darkness is that bad. It is terrible. And yes, it is more powerful than we are.

But still... "I fear no danger."

Not because evil is powerless. Not because I know I can handle it. Not because I can get by with a little help from a good crew.

I fear no danger... because God is with me.

Go ahead and read all of Psalm 23. It's well, well worth your time, whether you've never run into it before or you've got it memorized. Notice it says that "The LORD is my shepherd." You know who that Shepherd is? John 10:11 says, "'I am the good shepherd. The good shepherd lays down his life for the sheep.'" You know who's saying that?

Yep.

Jesus.

In other words, as you're walking through dangerous times, you can have confidence – not because it's not dangerous, but because your Shepherd has walked through this before. Jesus has been in this dark, dark valley, and he has faced all your enemies. And he let them take him out.

And then he conquered them. He even conquered death and walked out the other side... alive.

And now, no matter how scary it is, Jesus is walking with you. Sure, there are a lot of terrible things in this universe. And they are terrible. You can admit that.

Jesus is bigger. He is stronger. And he's at your side.

So all those stories that show the unbeatable aliens? If we were by ourselves, yes, we would surely fall.

But we are not alone.

Prayer: Jesus, Lord of Angel Armies, sometimes it appears that I have no hope. Remind me in those times that I am not alone. Hold me in the palm of your hand and deliver me, just as you promised you would. Amen.

See? SEE? Russia = Bad Guys; USA = Good Guys!

Some science fiction is used to make us think about our own world. Classic *Star Trek* was famous for it, though it's hardly alone. Look at those aliens who are mean to each other just because they look different! That's ridiculous! Oh. That's weird. We humans do the same thing, don't we? We're mean to each other just because we don't all look the same.

You could almost call using science fiction this way a "reverse parable."

See, while Jesus was on this planet, he told parables. These were earthly stories with spiritual meanings. He would take normal, everyday stuff – gardening, debts, hosting a party – and use them to reveal truths about how God works. Maybe the most famous of

With Jesus's stories, though... he constantly points to God's grace.

these is the story of the Prodigal Son (also called the Lost Son) from Luke 15:11-32. I encourage you to read it on your own.

It's just normal stuff. A son disappoints his father. Runs away. Is ashamed of what he's become. Comes back and asks to work to be let back into some form of relationship – just an employee of the family. He knows he doesn't deserve to be a son. But an employee? That he could do.

All pretty normal.

And then Jesus reveals the crazy part: The father won't let the son work his way back into the family. Instead, he welcomes him back with open arms and reinstates him as a son!

Jesus reveals how amazing the love of God the Father is by using everyday things to open our eyes to how good our God is.

Science fiction goes the opposite route: It uses stuff from "out there" to reveal stuff about our earthly life.

I'd encourage you to look into these messages that science fiction stories send. Are they good messages? Compare with what Jesus speaks. (Which means getting to know what Jesus speaks better and better!)

With Jesus's stories, though, it's pretty amazing – he constantly points to God's grace. He constantly points to how God welcomes sinners, how he forgives, how he longs for his children, no matter how bad they've been. No matter how good a science fiction story is, Jesus's stories are always better because of that message!

Prayer: Dear Jesus, thank you for telling stories. I love stories, too! Help me value the grace of your stories more than stories of science fiction, even as I enjoy the gifts of imagination you have given to your people. Amen.

Trope Three

They're not evil... they're just misunderstood!

"OTHER THAN THAT, HE'S A GOOD KITTY."

Trope 3: They're not evil... they're just misunderstood!

Just Saying Hi

Captain Devereaux knew something had to be wrong, but the deck plating on the bridge was just too comfy right now to worry about it.

Wait. Deck plating. Bridge.

He opened his eyes to flying sparks and smoke. Lieutenant Cannon stood by her console, screaming commands down to engineering. "I don't care what you can or can't do! We need to get out of here!"

The ship rocked again.

Oh. That's right. The asteroids that had surrounded the ship had started pounding against the hull. Devereaux had gone flying. Probably had a concussion now. Well, it didn't matter what he had if they didn't get the ship out of here soon. "Lieutenant. Sit-rep, please." His voice was more than a little scratchy.

"They've set up a sequence, sir. They're hitting us pretty much all over."

"Let me see the sequence."

The bridge rocked again, but they surfed the quake relatively easily this time around. Devereaux scanned the readout on his screen, trying to figure things out.

Cannon's fingers flew over her console. "There. Artillery, target that asteroid there. If we can shatter it under our barrage, we should be able to get out of the circle and start evasive maneuvers."

"Belay that." The captain offered a grim smile. "Cannon, set course for that stone. Right there. Ramming speed."

"Sir?"

"You heard me, Lieutenant. Ramming speed."

"That'll tear the ship apart!"

"I suspect it might. But it's that, or these rocks will pulverize us. We couldn't escape before; what makes you think they'd let us get away if we blow up their littlest brother? Right there. Ramming speed. Now."

"Aye." Cannon tapped in the commands. She opened the ship-wide comm. "All hands, brace for impact! More impacts!"

The engines whined. They weren't used to such a beating and took a moment to get online with the idea of increasing speed. The asteroid ahead of them loomed. The engines grew louder. Louder.

And then the asteroid gave them the lightest tap and matched their course and speed. No damage done.

Cannon blinked at the screen, at her readouts, back at the screen. "Captain?"

"They're giant living space rocks, Lieutenant. They greeted us in our language. How do you think they greet each other in theirs?"

She processed a moment. "By hitting each other."

"Yep. They weren't attacking; they just wanted to say hi."

A Misunderstood Trope

Sometimes the aliens aren't evil. Sometimes the orcs really aren't so bad. Sometimes they're just misunderstood.

In this trope, the bad guys really aren't so bad.

In this trope, the bad guys really aren't so bad. They look pretty imposing at first, but usually through communication of some kind, we discover it's all a big misunderstanding. That's really how they say "hi," or they're being forced to attack by some bigger bad guy we never saw before, or maybe they were just never taught how to say "please." Once the truth comes out, we can usually live together in some reasonable facsimile of peace.

Can't We All Just Get Along?

This trope proposes a problem: We have conflicts with one another. Maybe those conflicts come between crew members of the same ship, interstellar empires, or us and the dragons that keep stealing our sheep.

Well, I can't see anything wrong with saying that's a problem. Can you? It's true that we often have conflicts in this world. I really hate that – and I'm not pandering at all when I say that. When I know a conflict is approaching, either a conflict I need to initiate because of my calling as a pastor or one that I expect someone to initiate with me because I've done something they don't like, I physically shake. I hate conflict.

So, yeah. We have conflicts here. And that's a problem.

This trope suggests the solution to the problem is understanding. If we just understood each other, we could get rid of most conflict.

Which means... you need to find out what the truth is.

What do you think? Use your discernment here. Does this trope present reality?

Well, there's certainly some wisdom here. Have you ever been mad at a friend and then later found out you were really dumb for being angry at them? If you'd just taken the time to understand them from the beginning, you could have saved both of you a lot of heartache.

The Bible would agree. Proverbs 10:12 says, "Hatred stirs up conflicts, but love covers all offenses." And since as Christians we're called to love even our enemies, well, it makes sense we would "cover up the offenses" of our enemies by finding out if they really are offenses, right? Did you really intend to be that mean, or were you having a rough day? Did that alien race really mean to be that aggressive, or is that just how that culture shows respect?

1 Peter 4:8 says, "Above all, maintain constant love for one another, since love covers a multitude of sins." Again, we're urged to love one another.

> *Maybe that person you don't like really is just misunderstood.*

Maybe, if we're talking about love, we should just go to the big chapter on love, 1 Corinthians 13. Here's verses four through seven: "Love is patient, love is kind. Love does not envy, is not boastful, is not arrogant, is not rude, is not self-seeking, is not irritable, and does not keep a record of wrongs. Love finds no joy in unrighteousness but rejoices in the truth. It bears all things, believes all things, hopes all things, endures all things."

Love rejoices in the truth.

Which means... you need to find out what the truth is. So, when encountering an alien race, and it looks like they're really mean, find out the truth first. Maybe they're just oblivious. It means when the dragon is coming to steal gold, find out the truth. Maybe the dragon is taking back what's rightfully his. Find out the truth!

And I should note, it really doesn't take a Christian to figure any of this out. It's just a good principle to live by. Stephen Covey in his *The Seven Habits of Highly Effective People* lists, "Seek first to understand, then to be understood." Look, maybe that person you don't like really is just misunderstood. Take some time to find out. Listen to them. You might learn something.

So, yeah. Smart trope. Maybe they are just misunderstood.

Except when they're not.

Maybe It's More than a Misunderstanding

So, seek first to understand. It's a good principle. But if you do that, will you eliminate all conflict?

Yeah... no.

To be fair, only the most simplistic reading of the trope would claim that all conflict would suddenly vanish. The movie *How to Train Your Dragon* seemed to say that if we just sought to understand each other, dragons and humans could live in peace. And then in *How to Train Your Dragon 2*, a new villain appeared whom you could not reason with.

> *Understanding is a good first step, but it won't eliminate every problem.*

You don't need to be Christian to get that, while understanding can eliminate some conflict, it doesn't eliminate it all. So be wary if the story you're experiencing seems to advocate complete peace through mutual understanding. Understanding is a good first step, but it won't eliminate every problem.

And that's because we are fallen.

Genesis 6:5 says, "...the LORD saw that human wickedness was widespread on the earth and that every inclination of the human mind was nothing but evil all the time." Check out Romans 3:9-20. It doesn't paint a very pretty picture of humanity.

See, we are by nature sinful. We inherit this sinfulness from our parents. What that means is that we are naturally selfish. I want what I want. And what I want isn't always going to be good for you – especially if what you want is different from what I want. And if what you want conflicts with what I want, well, tough. You're not getting your way if I have anything to say about it.

Ah, but is it that way if we're in a story that involves non-humans? If we just understand dwarves, will we be able to hammer out this mining dispute? What about trying to prevent war with the Wookiees?

Sorry. These other species won't fare any better. Romans 8:22 says, "For we know that the whole creation has been groaning together with labor pains until now." When humans sinned, we didn't just bring the wages of sin on ourselves. We brought it on all creation. The entire universe fell when we fell.

Which means, even if we encounter other species out there, they'll be just as broken as we are. Possibly in very different ways, but just as broken. They will still have sin. They will still be naturally selfish. Even understanding each other will not guarantee peace.

We need something bigger.

Thankfully, as deep as our sin is, Jesus's mercy is deeper. When Jesus died, he died for all of us – every part that has been touched with sin. We have a problem that we can't solve... but Jesus has. Jesus understood us. He didn't think we were peachy-keen. He saw how selfish we were.

> *Thankfully, as deep as our sin is, Jesus's mercy is deeper.*

And he loved us anyway.

He came, knowing how dark this world could be. And he knew he would not be understood. He knew he would be rejected. He knew he would be executed.

He came anyway.

This is what we need first: Not to understand each other, but to see that we are understood, loved, and forgiven by Jesus.

So, what does all this have to do with the trope?

If the trope says that the solution to all our conflicts is understanding... that may well help with a single conflict, but it doesn't deal with why we have conflicts in the first place. It doesn't deal honestly with our sin and our need for a Savior. So even though it's good advice, we need to remember that there's something so much bigger that this trope doesn't address.

That said – it is still a good principle to live by. Try to understand your enemies. Listen to them. Maybe you'll find out that your differences aren't as big as you think they are. Maybe you do have more in common. After all, we're all sinners. We're all in the same boat.

Let's listen to each other.

Using Our Differences to Share Jesus

Look, what this trope teaches... do. The trope says we need to understand each other. Well, how well do you understand this other person you're talking to? You understand that this person needs Jesus just like you do. But do you understand who they are? What their dreams are? How has this broken world has scarred them? Do you see the wounds that they suffer from and know need healing? Listen to understand.

When you do that, it will help you understand where to show them Jesus. It will help you show that they have been broken by sin, just as you are. And it will help you show them Jesus, to share him as the answer to their problem.

Are You Pondering What I'm Pondering?

The next time you experience a story that, in the end, shows we need to understand each other, ask:

- ✓ Does this story seem to indicate that if we just understood each other, we could eliminate conflict? Or is that just how *this* conflict was solved?

- ✓ Why would merely understanding each other eliminate conflict?

- ✓ Is it possible to eliminate all conflict in any setting? Why or why not?

The next time you enjoy a story that shows that if we understand each other, we can eliminate conflict, ask:

- ✓ Do I seek first to understand?

- ✓ How can I listen better?

- ✓ Jesus tells us to love our enemies. He loved me, his enemy. Am I showing love to my enemies?

Meditations on Understanding

<u>Try to Understand</u>

It's been done a million times in stories. The two main characters are close friends, until a misunderstanding separates them. Maybe a bad guy planted evidence that one betrayed the other. Maybe it's an old mistake that tears them apart. In *The Return of the King*, if Frodo understood Sam better, he'd know that Sam would never betray him. He doesn't understand, though, and rejects his loyal friend.

> *See, the only person who loved the way it says in that Bible passage... was Jesus.*

It's probably happened a million times in your own life. There was a fight because someone didn't understand you.

Or maybe you didn't understand them.

1 Corinthians 13:4-7 says, "Love is patient, love is kind. Love does not envy, is not boastful, is not arrogant, is not rude, is not self-seeking, is not irritable, and does not keep a record of wrongs. Love finds no joy in unrighteousness but rejoices in the truth. It bears all things, believes all things, hopes all things, endures all things."

Do you love you friends? Your family?

That means you're not irritable. Have you ever been irritated with someone you love? Maybe because you don't understand what they're doing, or they don't understand what you're doing?

Love is patient. I know I'm not always patient with what my friends are doing. Sometimes they get under my skin.

I know I don't always "bear all things" that my family puts me through. I don't understand why whatever-it-is is such a big deal to them.

Maybe I don't love the way I should. If I did, I would seek to understand those close to me. That would eliminate a lot of conflict, wouldn't it?

Thank God I'm not judged on how much I love or how well I understand. Instead, Jesus was judged in my place. See, the only person who loved the way it says in that Bible passage... was Jesus. His love for me is still patient. It is still kind. It still isn't irritable. It still bears all things.

We are saved not because of *our* love, but because of *his*. We are forgiven for the many times we failed to love. We are washed clean.

And guess what? He loves your friends and family just as much. If Jesus takes the time to love and understand them... maybe you can do the same thing, huh? Not that it gets you something – you're already forgiven! – but because Jesus loves them, too.

Prayer: Dear Jesus, I don't always take the time to understand my friends and family. Forgive me. I know that you always understand me. Thank you. Help me to love the way you want me to love. Help me to try to understand those around me. Amen.

Love Your Klingons

Jesus says, "Love your enemies" (Luke 6:27). Does that include alien races bent on destroying you? Should Captain Kirk love the Klingons?

Babylon 5 has a great moment where, if humans had attempted to understand another alien race, it would have prevented war. Humans encountered a Minbari ship for the first time, and the ship approached with gunports open. In that culture, it was a sign of respect to do so. The humans misunderstood it as an act of aggression and opened fire, starting a bloody war that forms the background of the television series.

Imagine if the humans had attempted to understand first.

But understanding first is dangerous. It leaves you vulnerable. If the humans had attempted to understand why an unknown ship was approaching with open gunports first – what if the other ship opened fire? How were the humans to know they were coming in peace?

Seeking to understand first is a way to show love; and love itself is always risky. What if the other person doesn't love back? What if they use your vulnerability to strike at you, to embarrass you, to hurt you?

Love is always a risk. It's a risk that Jesus himself took for us. Romans 5:8 says, "But God proves his own love for us in that while we were still sinners, Christ died for us."

> *Love is always a risk. It's a risk that Jesus himself took for us.*

While we were still sinners.

Before we ever thought that we needed help. Before we ever would have considered that God himself would choose to rescue us. Before we turned from any wrong action or thought.

Jesus risked everything to love us. He gave himself. All of himself. Even to death on a cross.

Not everyone loves him back. Not everyone rejoices in what he's done. Not everyone thinks they need help.

Jesus risked it anyway and loved us that much. He loved his enemies... us.

(And yes – we were his enemies. Romans 8:7 says, "The mind-set of the flesh is hostile to God because it does not submit to God's law. Indeed, it is unable to do so.")

But Jesus made us friends. He loved us.

Now what he's done for us... he wants us to do for others. He wants us to be his hands in this world. To reach out and love our enemies, too. And that starts... with understanding. And understanding often starts with listening. Which is risky.

But Jesus thought you were worth the risk. So, you risk it for those around you.

Prayer: Jesus, thank you for risking everything to buy me back from my sin and make me a friend. Forgive me for the many times I didn't love my enemies. Change my heart so it reflects yours. Help me to love my enemies – the way you love me. Amen.

Not What You Were

Have you ever seen the movie *The Dark Crystal*? At the end of that movie, the evil Skeksis and the noble but impotent Mystics are driven together to change into a new, shining race: the urSkeks. Something evil and something impotent were totally changed into something new and better.

We were as bad as the Skeksis. Maybe not on the outside. Maybe no one else would have ever guessed. But on the inside, we were so bad God considered us dead: "And you were dead in your trespasses and sins in which you previously lived according to the ways of this world, according to the ruler of the power of the air, the spirit now working in the disobedient" (Ephesians 2:1-2).

You were dead. But you are not what you were.

"But God, who is rich in mercy, because of his great love that he had for us, made us alive with Christ even though we were dead in trespasses. You are saved by grace" (Ephesians 2:4-5)!

You're not dead anymore. You're alive! You're new!

Your new self? This is who you are now: No longer lost. Found. No longer rejected. Accepted. No longer sinner. Saint. This is your new identity.

And that means you don't have to look on your old self with nostalgia. An urSkeks from *The Dark Crystal* wouldn't look back on his time as a Skeksis and say, "Man, I miss that evil stuff. Life was so much better then."

> *You're not dead anymore. You're alive! You're new!*

There is a catch, though. You are a saint... but you still have a sinful nature. So, don't be surprised if you continue to struggle with sin. Continue to fight it – that's not who you are anymore. So why should you continue to live in sin? That part of you is dead. Why hang out with a dead person? Confess your sin, confident that Jesus forgives you. And use that knowledge of who you are – someone new – to walk away from the old self.

And then... also don't be surprised when other people continue to sin, even after they know Jesus. You are a saint. You have a sinful nature. So do they! But if they're Christian, they're alive.

And you? You're alive, too.

Prayer: Jesus, I know that you have made me alive. Thank you. So often I forget that I am not what I was. Help me to remember my new identity as I deal with others. Help me to not be surprised by sin, but to rejoice in your forgiveness. Amen.

Trope Four

Don't Interfere with Alien Cultures

Trope 4: Don't Interfere with Alien Cultures

The Directive is Not Prime

Of course, the place was already inhabited by some other freaky species. Why wouldn't it be?

"We got every right to this rock! I paid for my stake, and I ain't leavin'!" one enlightened soul bellows from the back of the barn we all sit in.

Yeah. A barn. Look, I know back on Earth you can have all those fancy council rooms and all that, but out here on the frontier it's a little different. We put up the buildings we have to first, and then we add in all those luxuries later. Eventually.

Anyway, the chairwoman, she slams her little hammer thing on the table once and just stares out into the crowd. We all calm down pretty quick. I think maybe she was a teacher or something before moving out here; she's got a way with crowds that only someone dealing with a roomful of kids has. "We all paid, Maddock. We all paid everything we had. But the directive is clear: We are not to interfere with any primitive civilization. We will be sending a message to Earth to request relocation. We should get the reply within three years, same as every other message. So until then, nicely keep yourselves away from the locals."

I raise a hand.

Good ol' chairwoman nods in my direction. "Mr. Thornton, so recently arrived from Earth, do you have something to add?"

"How about we don't?" I ask.

She raises her eyebrows. I feel everyone looking at me.

"Look, I'm not saying we kick the Grebs off whatever they claim is theirs. We've done enough crap like that to each other back home. I'm just saying... why don't we try living together for a little bit before we ask to be lifted off this rock? We all paid enough. Let's put in the effort."

There are general nods of assent.

"Mr. Thornton, what you propose violates the terms of our charter." Wow. Her voice was like ice. Definitely a teacher. She's going to try putting me in a corner and calling my parents next.

"Maybe it's a dumb charter," I counter.

Yeah, ok, maybe that wasn't the best counter to her argument. Now I'm locked up in another barn. This one smells a little funny.

But it's okay. I've got some buddies coming to spring me.

The ground in front of me shifts, and these two Grebs haul themselves out of the dirt like they're crawling out of a swimming pool. They come over and untie my wrists. One winks at me.

Charter says we shouldn't interfere?

Too late. They're interfering with us, and I don't mind a bit.

A Trope of Important Directives

You leave a culture alone to develop at its own pace.

This is a trope I've never seen in fantasy, though I'm sure someone can find a solid example of it somewhere. In many science fiction shows, though, there's this idea: You leave a culture alone to develop at its own pace.

Maybe it's alien races visiting Earth right now, but they don't make themselves known because they want us to do what we're going to do without interference. Maybe it's us centuries in the future not messing around with aliens who haven't made it off their own planets yet so they can reach out in their own way.

Any which way, make sure you don't interfere with alien cultures.

Pollution is the Worst

This trope targets a problem: We pollute other cultures with our own. We've seen it plenty on this planet in our history. The US sets up military bases in foreign lands. Suddenly the area around the base starts looking more and more like the States – or at least approximating it. It doesn't look like it used to. Google "Tourism in Goa," and you'll see an area that has been devastated by what many call "cultural pollution."

Basically, when one culture encounters another, both are affected. However, the weaker culture is often left off worse. Maybe it's dirty water or litter or the evaporation of centuries-old morals. Maybe it's all the children abandoning old traditions.

That's a real-world problem that can be translated into science fiction so very well. If advanced aliens landed on Earth, wouldn't it change so much of how our world works?

The assumption "All cultures are equal" often stretches to mean, "All religions are equal."

So, this trope basically says: An advanced civilization will pollute less-advanced civilizations, but should seek to avoid doing so. That presents an interesting assumption. Why shouldn't we change other cultures? Because all cultures are equal.

What do you think? Are all cultures equal?

The Bible clearly states that all *people* are equal. Romans 3:23-24 says, "For all have sinned and fall short of the glory of God. They are justified freely by his grace through the redemption that is in Christ Jesus." All people are equally sinful and equally in need of Jesus. All people are equally saved only by Jesus taking their punishment in their place on the cross. That's what grace is, by the way: love that is undeserved. We didn't deserve God's love, but he loved us anyway. He loved us so much he chose to die for us.

In some ways, this assumption that cultures are equal isn't bad. We are all equal in that need for a Savior!

But here's the other side of that coin: The assumption "All cultures are equal" often stretches to mean, "All religions are equal."

Is that true? Do all religions admit that we can't save ourselves? Do all religions point out that we are justified, that we are declared not guilty, because God sent his Son to die in our place? I don't know any religion that teaches that other than Christianity.

In other words, though every culture has some things to admire, every culture has also been infected by sin. Sometimes that sin is easy to see; sometimes it's not. But because every culture has been infected by sin, every culture needs the answer to sin: Jesus.

> *We're all equal. We are all equally sinful.*

And that means that not every religion is equal. A religion that doesn't have Jesus may be quaint. It may sense echoes of God's plan. But if it doesn't have Jesus dying for sinners, it doesn't have what we need.

So, this assumption that we are all equal has some good aspects, but also possibly a dangerous one.

We are Not the Champions

We're only going to touch on this briefly here, but often times in science fiction, there can also be this idea that we shouldn't interfere with other cultures because they're pristine. After all, if we touch this theoretical other culture, we pollute them! Does that indicate that we're worse than them?

I'm going to reiterate: we're all equal. We are all equally sinful. We are all equally in need of a Savior. Sin may infect that other culture in a different way, and maybe we see that as "better." I'll tell you, there are certainly some aspects of ancient cultures I'm attracted to over what we face today. Sometimes I think I'd love to be a Jedi (or at least have Force powers). But whether you're in the Republic, the Empire, or the First Order, every culture has been infected by sin. We're not better, and neither are they.

We all need Jesus.

Just Leave Them Alone

This trope assumes that we will pollute other cultures with our own. What's the solution? Why, let them develop on their own. If you're a Trekkie, you've probably seen this especially in episodes that feature the Prime Directive. Pre-warp civilizations are to be left alone! Most of the time, the show will display the captain ignoring or bending that rule! There's a reason why: Even in an often-picture-perfect world like *Star Trek*, there's this inkling that maybe the idea of "leave them alone" isn't great.

And it's not great.

Let me prove it: Does "leave them alone" show love? Does denying medical care or clean water show love?

I think most people would agree that getting people what they need for basic living would be the loving thing to do. There's a reason that most people want to support humanitarian efforts!

Does it show love for souls to leave them alone when they don't have Jesus?

Remember, Jesus claims "I am the way, the truth, and the life. No one comes to the Father except through me" (John 14:6). If no one introduces a group of people to Jesus... they won't find their way to the Father any other way.

While it's true that cultures do pollute each other, and it's true that often we affect each other in terrible ways, we still want to show love. We still want to reach out with the best thing: Jesus.

Using "Leave Them Alone" to Share Jesus

Think about saying this to someone else:

"Do you think that another civilization might want some of the things we could offer them? Like, do you think a primitive culture might want medical care or clean water or air conditioners?

What if we had a resource that could let them live forever without sorrow and no overpopulation? Would that be worthwhile to offer?"

Are You Pondering What I'm Pondering?

The next time you experience a story that uses "Leave that culture alone," ask these questions:

- ✓ Does this story say that it's *good* to leave other cultures alone, or is it simply using that rule as backdrop to tell a story?

- ✓ Does this story assume that all cultures are equal or that any contact would harm another civilization? In what ways does the story assume that all cultures are equal?

- ✓ Does this story assume that withholding necessary humanitarian aid would actually somehow be good?

The next time you enjoy a story that uses "Leave that culture alone," ask these questions:

- ✓ Do I think all cultures are equal? In what ways?

- ✓ What are good ways to interfere with another culture? What would be some bad ways?

- ✓ What are ways we can respect other cultures while still sharing Jesus with them?

If no one introduces a group of people to Jesus... they won't find their way to the Father any other way.

Meditations on "Leave Them Alone"

God Violates the Prime Directive

> *Unlike when human civilizations mess with each other, though, there was no negative to what Jesus did.*

Leave less advanced civilizations alone. When you mess with them, you change them forever, and not for the better. It's better for everyone if you just stay separate.

That's what a lot of science fiction would have you believe.

God disagrees.

God is way more advanced than we are. Isaiah 55:8-9 tells us that God says, "For my thoughts are not your thoughts, and your ways are not my ways... For as heaven is higher than earth, so my ways are higher than your ways, and my thoughts than your thoughts."

Need some evidence, and not just talk? All right. God can convert his words into matter. In the beginning, he created everything by just speaking it into being. God has mastered the art of being nonlinear; he's not bound by time. He's mastered the art of being nonlocal; he's not in any one specific location. In fact, he's everywhere. Oh, and he also knows everything. Anything you know, he knows better, in far more true a way than you can fathom.

As I said, way more advanced than we are.

But God didn't say, "Well, I'll wait until they catch up to me." He knew we couldn't catch up to him. In our sin, we would only spiral further and further down into darkness. He didn't say, "Leave that primitive people alone."

God interfered. He stepped into time. He stepped into space. He joined us and became one of us. He changed all human history by redeeming us from our sin. He changed us forever.

Unlike when human civilizations mess with each other, though, there was no negative to what Jesus did. He didn't leave behind lots of litter or encourage people to abandon any good traditions. Instead, he loved us – no matter what culture we are. And he loved us enough to take our sins away. He loved us enough to interfere and give us the best thing ever: eternal life in a land with no sorrow.

That's better than anything my or any other culture could ever give me.

So yeah. Be glad that God didn't say, "Well, they're not advanced enough. I won't interfere with them." He follows a different prime directive: love.

Prayer: God, thank you for interfering with us on Earth. Though your thoughts are so much above ours, you still chose to come and rescue us from our sins and from death. Thank you, Jesus. Help me to praise you for your interference! Amen.

What Culture is God?

One of the names the Bible gives Jesus is "Immanuel." It literally means, "God with us."

Have you ever considered what it means that God is with us?

In a lot of science fiction stories, if aliens visit earth, they aren't really "with us." They might settle among us. They might share technology. But they're not really "with us." In the 90's television show *Earth: Final Conflict*, the alien Taelon mostly settle on the moon, outside of Earth's political sphere, but they do grow a few embassies on Earth. They try to interact with humans but are so different they always stand out. I think that approach is pretty common in science fiction. Aliens are, well, alien, and they're not really "with us."

That's not what Jesus did. Isaiah 53:2 says, "He didn't have an impressive form or majesty that we should look at him, no appearance that we should desire him." When God became human, he looked like any one of us.

> Have you ever considered what it means that God is with us?

In stories where aliens visit Earth, you can usually tell that something's up even if they look like us. They don't act like us. They don't understand our culture.

Jesus, though? He grew up a part of Israelite culture during the Roman occupation. He went to synagogue on Sabbath. He ate what everyone else ate. He spoke their language. Jesus joined their culture.

Aliens land, and they change culture by their very appearance. Jesus, though? He didn't seek to change our culture.

He sought to change us.

He wasn't afraid to call sin, sin. He wasn't afraid to call it out, whether it was someone everyone else looked down on or those in the height of power. He knew that everyone needed what he was about to offer.

And then he offered them himself. He gave himself on the cross.

And those who trust this sacrifice, those who know that Jesus died for them, they are changed forever. They are no longer members of this world; now they belong to heaven.

You belong to heaven.

Jesus belonged to a culture on Earth, yes, but his goal wasn't changing the culture. He lived inside the culture to save *you*. He did that as your substitute – to win you for heaven.

Prayer: Jesus, thank you for being my substitute and even living inside a culture for me. Help me to live in my culture while still belonging to you. Amen.

Should We Change Culture?

I'm going to say something that hopefully doesn't overly shock you:

Slavery is wrong.

Okay, you breathing again? I know that was a hard thing to read.

Sometimes science fiction shows pick really obvious morals like that. "Slavery is bad." Well, thanks for that cutting-edge commentary, random sci-fi show!

> *Jesus died for the slave who needed rescue, and he died for the owner who needed rescue just as much.*

However, it wasn't always so obvious. In the first century, slavery was simply a way of life. Paul, a man God used to write about half the New Testament, was in prison for sharing Jesus. And while there, he encountered a runaway slave who belonged to a Christian. And while that slave was near Paul, God used Paul to tell this slave about his sin, and the man who saved him from his sin – Jesus.

But now Paul had a problem: He had a Christian slave who belonged to a Christian owner. What to do now? Should he attempt to change the entire culture and make it so everyone knew that slavery was wrong, or should he just keep his mouth shut and not interfere?

Paul wrote a letter. I'm not going to quote it here; I want you to go read it. It's short. It's the book of Philemon. (Even if you know your Bible well, you may need the table of contents to find it – like I said, it's short and easy to miss!)

Did Paul ever say slavery was wrong in that entire book?

Nope!

It's crazy, right? Shouldn't the whole thing be telling this slave owner to release all his slaves?

Did Paul mind his own business about the issue, though?

Nope! He didn't do that either!

Instead, Paul talks about how brothers and sisters in Christ prize one another. The relationship is different now because Jesus died for them both. He died for the slave who needed rescue, and he died for the owner who needed rescue just as much. That puts them both on an even playing field.

And if it's an even playing field, is it right to hold that person as a slave?

See, Paul does something different. Instead of aiming to transform culture, he urges a single person to view his fellow human as Jesus sees him.

Now imagine if everyone viewed each other as Jesus views us: sinners that he died for.

I think that would be pretty awesome.

Yeah, if you want to change culture... change a person. Show them Jesus. And then help them see everyone else as Jesus sees them.

Prayer: Jesus, it is so hard for me to see people the way you see them. I complain about my culture and want to change it, but it's so hard to change something that big. Change my heart to see other people the way you see them. Use me to change someone's heart near me so that they know you and start seeing other people the way you see them. And then use me to change someone else's heart. And someone else's. Until you bring me home. Amen.

Trope Five

Evolution

PROFESSOR BIGFOOT FINDS THE MISSING LINK.

Trope 5: Evolution

Evolution Gives, Evolution Takes Away...

The ground in front of me shifts, and these two Grebs haul themselves out of the dirt like they're crawling out of a swimming pool. They come over and untie my wrists. One winks at me.

Charter says we shouldn't interfere?

Too late. They're interfering with us, and I don't mind a bit.

I bow to them. "Thanks, gents. I appreciate it. Now, mind if I hitch a ride outta here?"

They look a little like shrews with four extra tunneling arms, and they stand about six foot tall. One looks at me and struggles to speak in English. "They will not stay?"

"Nope. They're idiots."

"Idiots?"

I try to remember their saying. "They're digging through air."

It blinks. "Then you will come with us." It stretches one of its many hands toward me and gestures for me to hold on to it.

And then we're swimming through dirt.

The first time this happened, I wasn't expecting it and tried screaming.

Look, if you're swimming through dirt, don't scream. You'll be picking earthworms out of your teeth for weeks. It tastes horrible. Oh, and it might suffocate you a little.

We finally surface a few miles out of town. It is insane how fast these buggers go. I cough a little – look, you try not breathing when all you feel is dirt shoving past your face! – anyway, I cough a little and look at them as they sit half-submerged in the dirt. "How did you guys get to do that dirt thing anyway?"

One blinks, processing my words. These guys are smart, way smarter than we are, which is why I want to stick around. They could teach us a lot.

But when he speaks, I think maybe I was wrong about the smart thing. "When we walked on land, we were hunted and burned by the sun. Deity changed us, blessed us, and helped us to run fast where we would be safe."

"Right." I shake my head. The crazy buggers. These Grebs were perfectly adapted for this planet. So much of it was loose dirt. They could hunt for anything from under the ground, eat it, and get away. There weren't any predators that could find them if they were underground. But apparently, they didn't think much of themselves if they wanted to credit some "Deity" for their success here.

"Are you cursed? Is that why you do not run fast underneath?"

I huffed a laugh. "Look, we evolved to be apex predators on our planet. We never needed to run fast underneath."

"Evolved? Does that mean your deity did not give you what you needed?"

An Evolving Trope

This trope assumes that all life in the universe can be traced back to single cells that came together purely by chance. Such settings usually assume a materialistic universe.

Not every story that presupposes evolution defies any kind of spiritual reality, but it is common.

Wait a second. What do I mean by "materialistic"? Am I saying that the universe really likes stuff?

No. "Materialistic" in this case means that matter is all that exists. If you cannot measure it in some way, it does not exist. There are no such things as souls; there's only the firing of your brain. There's no such thing as God or spirits. They're made up, or they're natural phenomena that are being explained in superstitious terms.

Not every story that presupposes evolution defies any kind of spiritual reality, but it is common.

Anyway, the trope assumes that all life came together and descends from a single cell, whether on this planet or another.

Where did We All Come From?

This trope asks a very profound question: Where did we all come from?

Now, I'm not going to go deep into this question. There is *so much* great information out there; I'd recommend *The Case for a Creator* by Lee Strobel as a good place to start. If you're looking for something way more science-y that's not Christian at all but makes you go "Hm," let me recommend *The Structure of Scientific Revolutions* by Thomas S. Kuhn. Kuhn's book is very challenging and not for the faint of heart – head's up!

Let me lay out my stance very simply: The book of Genesis says that God created the world in six roughly twenty-four-hour periods. According to that account, he did so in an order that defies any modern understanding of evolution. Go ahead; check out the first chapter of Genesis and compare to any modern textbook. He told creatures to reproduce according to their "kinds." (Not species – God left room for some genetic drift, but not so much that one "kind" becomes another.) I trust that God said what he meant.

Not only did God create us, but he continues to be involved in this world.

You won't find that very often in science fiction, unless you pick up a distinctly Christian science fiction book. And even then, the proposed answer to "Where did we come from?" might try to incorporate evolution. It might propose that a spiritual force guided evolution and so somehow both can be true. In fact, there are plenty of people who believe that, but how the Bible paints creation (and not just in Genesis 1) makes it pretty much impossible to say, "The Bible is true" and still hold to evolution.

Most science fiction, however, will ignore any spiritual reality altogether. The question is why? What's the big deal with evolution? Why would we want to make it possible to ignore any kind of spiritual reality?

Well, if there's something out there, if there's something that we owe our existence to, it's probably a lot bigger and a lot smarter than us. But if we came about by chance, if there's nothing guiding us into being, we don't have to answer to anyone. We got us, and that's enough.

Again, the Bible claims something very different: Not only did God create us, but he continues to be involved in this world. He didn't just wind up the universe and walk off to munch on a microwave burrito. He's actually watching not just the universe as a whole, but *you*, too. The God who created you cares about what you do.

And he's not pleased by what he sees.

That's terrifying, isn't it? If something is powerful enough to design an atom and string together how gravity functions, if that something looks at you and is displeased, that something can wipe you out so, so easily.

But he doesn't.

Instead, he steps into time, into his universe, becoming one of us, *human*, and rescues us from our sins. That's crazy.

But it means nothing if he's not the one who designed and made us in the first place.

What that means is... when all those science fiction shows assume evolution, well, I'll say they're making a very faulty assumption. Their answer to, "Where did we all come from?" is the wrong answer.

Where Did All the Aliens Come From Then, Huh?

A lot of stories will use evolution as the answer to a similar but different problem: Where did all the aliens come from?

Let's say we're in a story where aliens exist. If we hold to the Bible, then we have a God who created those aliens. That creates some challenges. Does that mean that every race also fell when Adam and Eve chose to sin? Does that mean Jesus has to rescue each alien species? While a Klingon Jesus would be entertaining, I have a hard time imagining him. Would that mean that other species maybe haven't fallen into sin, as C. S. Lewis postulates in *The Space Trilogy*?

On the other hand, if we just say everything is random, well, life randomly developed on other planets. Problem solved. Now we can have aliens, no questions asked!

While it does make for simpler storytelling, I need to ask: For most stories you encounter, does answering the question, "Where do aliens come from?" really matter to the story being told? Most stories aren't about where we're from.

> *If we hold to the Bible, then we have a God who created those aliens.*

In other words, for a lot of science fiction, even if evolution plays a part in the background of the story, it probably doesn't matter to the overall narrative. I enjoy a *lot* of *Star Trek* even though it normally assumes materialistic evolution. In other words, often enough, don't sweat it. I remember when I was growing up, every time a show mentioned "millions of years ago" my parents would simply roll their eyes. I got the point; they were going to enjoy the show while tossing out this part they didn't agree with.

Granted, some science fiction stories really do focus on that. David Brin's Uplift series (featuring a great novel entitled *Startide Rising*) proposes a universe where every thinking species was raised up from a non-thinking species by some sort of patron race. No one knows where humans came from, causing some consternation in the universe. *Star Trek: The Next Generation* has an episode entitled "The Chase" that finally explains why all those aliens look like humans: They're all descended from another older race that seeded the galaxy long ago. Michael Crichton's book *The Lost World* felt like an advertisement for evolution even when I read it when it first came out, denying any kind of spiritual existence.

If you hold that evolution didn't happen... is that sort of story something you want to read? Is that something that is "good"?

When I was younger, I read one story that centered on evolution. The book was *Tom Swift: The DNA Disaster* by F. Gwynplaine MacIntyre (writing under the name Victor Appleton). The entire book centered on a gun that basically sends living beings further back the evolutionary scale. I loved that book. I loved seeing normal things transform. A cat becomes a saber-toothed tiger? Of course, I want to read about that! (If you're a *Phineas and Ferb* fan, you've seen Doctor Doofenshmirtz perfect a similar device. Well, perfect is probably too strong a word.)

Anyway, I knew that what I was reading was wrong. So what did I do? I explained to my dad, "This story takes place in a universe where evolution is true."

And that was that. My fiction remained fiction, and I knew that it wasn't fact.

Make sure if you're taking in science fiction that focuses on evolution, you can keep your facts from your fiction.

An Assumption That Isn't So Special

There's another problem with evolution that we need to talk about.

Science fiction that populates the universe with so many other aliens often has to tackle a different problem: What makes humans so special?

If we're all descended from muck, if we're all just adapted to live in our various environments, are we all just the same, whether we're Wookiee or Narn or Vulcan or Goa'uld?

If evolution is true, we may all be made of starstuff, but no race is any different from any other. That's why in so many science fiction settings, humans have to prove they're "better" in some way. We're more innovative or scrappy, or we learn fast or something. In *Doctor Who*, for example, the Doctor often expresses his love of humanity because we keep exploring. That's what makes us special.

There's a problem with that, though. If what makes us special is what we do, does that mean we're not special when we stop doing it?

The Bible tells us something different. It tells us that we are special because God made us special. We are special because God loves us. And since God doesn't change, his love won't change. That means that we are special. Period. We can't lose that specialness. It doesn't matter if you're a superhero or a quadriplegic; you are still special.

> We are special because God loves us.

Using Evolution to Share Jesus

First, there are *so many* resources if this is of interest to you. I'd recommend you checking out answersingenesis.org. While I don't advocate for everything they write – they generally focus too much on Law and not nearly enough on Gospel – they are still a good resource to know and visit.

However, if you want a slightly different way to talk about evolution to share Jesus, imagine saying this:

"Have you ever noticed that in a good story everything fits together? I mean, when there's a good story, you know that something you hear about in the beginning is going to come back, right? That's when you know there's a good storyteller.

"Do you think the world works that way? Everything fits together? The ecosystems are amazing how everything works together! It sounds to me like the world needs a storyteller, then. Someone that came up with the story from the beginning.

"And I know who that storyteller is, and the amazing way he joined our story... Let me tell you about Jesus."

Are You Pondering What I'm Pondering?

The next time you experience a story that uses evolution, ask these questions:

✓ Is the inclusion of evolution necessary to this story?

✓ Does this story assume that if there is a spiritual reality, it's easily ignored?

✓ Why does this story assume evolution?

✓ What does this story claim makes humanity special? Can that quality be lost?

The next time you enjoy a story that uses evolution, ask these questions:

✓ How do I keep the "reality" of the story separate from the reality of God's truth?

✓ What do I think makes me special? Is it possible to lose that thing? What does God say makes me special?

✓ What attracted me to this story? Why did I enjoy it? Do those reasons have anything to do with evolution as portrayed in the story? If so, what do I need to be aware of in myself?

Children of the Atom, Children of God

In both the comics and the movies about the X-Men, mutants are the next step in human evolution. One of the constant back-and-forths in the series deals with what to do with humans. If mutants really are the next step, doesn't that make "flatscan" humans... obsolete? At least worth less?

Of course, the X-Men are the good guys, and they argue that of course normal humans are still of worth! In fact, in their history, the X-Men have often had some very strong human allies.

But... if mutants really are the next step, doesn't it make sense that humans should be allowed to die off? Doesn't it make sense that the next step be allowed to take the next step?

> *We are worthy because our Father loved us enough to send his Son to die for us.*

If our worth is in what we contribute, absolutely. Humans can't do as much as mutants. I know I don't have incredible regeneration skills or telekinetic abilities. I'd love to have powers like that, but the most impressive thing I can do is make people hallucinate by writing down stories for them to read.

But if our worth isn't in what we contribute, where is our worth?

In the Bible there was a man who realized he wasn't worth anything. He had wasted half his father's fortune and was penniless. He planned to say to his father, "I'm no longer worthy to be called your son. Make me like one of your hired workers" (Luke 15:19). He could contribute nothing; maybe he could labor enough to get a paycheck.

But his father cast that aside and threw his son a party. He was so excited. You see, what made the son worthy wasn't what he contributed to his father; it was his Father's love for him.

Humans are worthwhile not because of what we bring to society, not because of our abilities or talents. We are worthy because our Father loved us enough to send his Son to die for us.

What if mutants suddenly start appearing and you're not one of them? Don't worry. You're still worthy because you don't determine your worth. Jesus does.

Prayer: Lord, thank you for making me worthy by loving me. When I feel that I'm not worth anything, please point me back to you. Remind me that my worth does not depend on me or my accomplishments. Amen.

Um... But the World Looks Old.

Maybe you've noticed. The world is millions of years old.

But that doesn't track if what the Bible says is true. You can't have millions of years with plants and not a single animal or even the sun. (Compare with the order that Genesis 1 says God created the world.)

Instead of a newborn planet, God created a stable world that was ready for life.

But... if you carbon date rocks, they're old!

So what do we do?

It's actually a lot easier than you might think. Take a look at Genesis 2. God creates Adam and Eve, both on day six of creation. They're just a few hours old when Adam sees Eve and spouts love poetry: "This one, at last, is bone of my bone and flesh of my flesh; this one will be called 'woman,' for she was taken from man" (Genesis 2:23).

You ever hang out with someone just a few hours old? They're not normally spouting love poetry. At best they're spouting some wails, waiting to be fed.

And then God *gives* Adam and Eve to each other, and there's the first marriage! And they're only a few hours old!

But these aren't newborns. They may be only a few hours old, but they have the *appearance* of adults. They have the bodies of adults. They have the brains of adults. For all intents and purposes, they *are* adults, even though they've only existed for a few hours!

Why would God do that? Well, he wanted to create people who could live. The best way to do that would be to create them as adults so they could take care of themselves and each other. In other words, God knew what would work best and created Adam and Eve with the appearance of age because that's what would work best in this newborn creation.

Now apply that to the rest of the world. God knew creating a newborn planet probably wouldn't work well if he put Adam and Eve on it. From what we can tell, newborn planets are not really welcoming to human life. Or any life. So instead of a newborn planet, God created a stable world that was ready for life. He created a planet with the appearance of age because he cared enough about us that he wanted a place that would welcome us.

And if God set up all creation so that it would be hospitable to us, think about how much he must love you to put you someplace that is right for you. A place with the oxygen you need. A place with the food you need.

Even a place with his Word, so you get to know him.

That God is pretty cool, huh?

Prayer: Lord, thank you for creating a world that welcomes me. Thank you for creating me just right. Amen.

Let's Pretend He Doesn't Exist.

Our sinful natures like things that let us ignore God. Maybe it's setting up a worldview that says if God exists, then he has nothing to do with how the universe runs. Maybe it's feeding us the lie that says, "I'm pretty decent; only people with problems need things like a church." Any way they can do it, our sinful natures love ignoring God.

Why is that?

Don't ignore this message... It gives you eternal life.

Well, if you ignore someone, you probably don't have a good relationship with that person, do you? If you're ignoring someone, are you going to listen to them? Of course not!

That's one of the reasons why people are so busy these days. Their sinful natures will get busy doing anything, because if you're busy, you have an excuse to ignore other people, and ultimately God himself. "Oh, sorry, can't talk about that. I need to get going." And how much more if you have a worldview that says that spiritual things, if they exist at all, don't affect you?

But... spiritual things do affect us, and they will affect us in huge ways. Doesn't matter if you don't think they exist. "Just as it was in the days of Noah, so it will be in the days of the Son of Man: People went on eating, drinking, marrying and giving in marriage until the day Noah boarded the ark, and the flood came and destroyed them all" (Luke 17:26-27).

In Noah's day, everyone ignored what Noah said. He was just some cranky old man anyway. And then the Flood came and destroyed them all.

Your sinful nature wants you destroyed. And it will do that by trying to get you to ignore what God says.

And what does God say?

You are a sinner. While you were still a sinner, Christ Jesus died for you. (Check out Romans 5:8!) Because of him, you are now a child of God. You belong in his family, and he is coming to take you home. You didn't do anything to help. Jesus did it all.

Don't ignore this message. It's not something that doesn't affect you. It gives you eternal life.

Oh, and maybe share it, too! Just as tricky as your sinful nature is, so is everyone else's! So, encourage people who already know Jesus, and try to show how he does affect your life... even now.

Prayer: Father, forgive me for ignoring you so often. My sinful nature tricks me, and I fall for it. Help me to look to you as the source of everything good in my life, especially my connection to Jesus. Amen.

Trope Six

The Quest

Trope 6: The Quest

Only One Can Save Us

The man pushed his way into the Assembly of Kings, gasping, hand pressed against his side. "Pellinor has fallen!" He collapsed. His hands left bloody stains on the marble floor.

I yelped.

Aramath glared at me.

I felt my cheeks redden at the wizard's glare, but it's not every day you see some man die like that. Well, at least I'd never seen anyone die like that. Most of the time girls are kept far from the battlefield, and that was fine with me. I liked baking. Baking and battlefields don't belong together.

No one heard my yelp, though. The kings were muttering to each other, drawing back into their little cliques.

They left the man there on the ground. No one cared about him. No one cared about the man who had died to bring them this news.

I scooted forward, bit by bit. Aramath had told me to keep myself small. No one was supposed to notice a girl in the Assembly, but I couldn't ignore the fallen man.

The muttering of the kings grew to a roar as they argued.

I didn't know what Pellinor was, and I didn't care. Who could care about some far-away place if you didn't care about the pain right in front of you?

I finally drew myself forward enough to kneel next to the fallen soldier. I put my hand against his cheek.

Still warm. Hot, like bread just out of the oven.

"Do not panic!" The wizard's voice broke through the commotion. "We yet have hope!"

The kings stopped their conferences. Every eye rested on the man who had brought me here.

The fallen man, though. He was still breathing.

The wizard continued, "One of my order foresaw the coming scourge. He knew we could not stand. He withdrew to a mountain keep to develop an incantation that would protect us all. He succeeded but died in his success. Only someone of his blood may enter his keep and speak the spell into reality."

I gently removed the man's helmet. His eyes fluttered. I didn't know what to do. What do you do with a bleeding man in an Assembly of Kings? You'd think kings would know better!

One of those kings shouted, "Someone the blood of a wizard? We all know wizards can't sire children! The spells you work destroy that ability!"

"Unless, young king, he had a child before he became a wizard." Aramath smiled. "Such a person would need to be escorted to the mountain keep, though. The journey is perilous, and time is of the essence."

"If it would protect the human kingdoms, such a man would have my protection!" Another man joined that cry. Another.

Aramath pointed at me. "Here she is. Salaya, daughter of Peridmath!"

I looked up at the kings. "We need to help this man! Quickly!" If they couldn't help someone right in front of them, what hope was there for some larger plan? I wasn't moving. I was going to help.

A Questing Trope

The hero needs to go do a thing! To do the thing, the hero needs to go somewhere far away and overcome obstacles and then find the thing or become better somehow and succeed in his or her goal! It's a quest!

We all want to feel important in some way.

This trope focuses on a hero's journey to succeed in some goal. The quest could be to destroy a ring or find an enemy's weakness or acquire a secret weapon. Quests can happen just about anywhere; they could be in a fantasy realm, a science fiction story, or even here and now.

Expect a hero to grow and change. The hero is vital to some big doings in the setting, and should the hero fail in his or her quest, it's likely that a lot of people will get hurt. Thus, the hero has a purpose that keeps him or her going even in the darkest of times. Often, the hero is accompanied by others, though not necessarily.

Whatever happens, you can bet that if it's a good quest, it's going to be an epic story.

You're Not the Hero

You are bound up in the ultimate battle between good and evil.

We all want to feel important in some way. We all want to be part of something bigger. And when you read a story about a quest, you see someone who really is part of something so much bigger. Maybe they've been sent by a king to do something that will change everything. Maybe they're part of some sort of fellowship. And those taking part in the quest have a purpose. In fact, there's probably some serious stakes, too. Perhaps, if they fail the entire world will fall to darkness.

Do you ever experience a story where you wish you lived in a world like that? Where there's a clear purpose, and you're bound up in it? Sure, even if the characters observe that they wish things were easier, and you'd probably say the same thing if you were there, you still long to have that kind of setup.

Well... do you have a purpose? Are you a part of something bigger?

Yes. You are.

You are bound up in the ultimate battle between good and evil. No, it's not that the orcs are attempting to conquer Chicago (or wherever you live). It's not that the Archmage of Cincinnati just unearthed a powerful artifact and now we have no hope.

It's far, far worse than that.

You see, we have a good and powerful King. Now, I suspect you already know where I'm going with this, but have you ever considered: In all the stories where there happens to be a good king, the king is addressed as "Lord"? There's a reason. A Lord is someone who rules, to whom people owe obedience.

And if you happen to be Christian, perhaps you've prayed to "the Lord." There's a reason: He rules, and we owe him obedience. In fact, every time you call him Lord, you're confessing that he is in charge of your life.

And if you're Christian, you also know that he is a good Lord. Sure, in fantasy, all the time there's evil kings. You could probably say that there's been some evil politicians in our times, too. In a lot of science fiction there are evil rulers. (I'm looking at you, Emperor Palpatine.) But in a lot of stories, there's also good kings. King Richard returns at the end of *Robin Hood*. King Arthur leads the Knights of the Round Table. The Starks in *Game of Thrones* are decent rulers! Aragorn, after some prodding, returns as the king in the aptly titled *The Return of the King*.

And what makes them good?

They are willing to fight for justice. They lead their people. They protect their people, often at a great price.

And that's what Jesus did.

Matthew 9:36 says, "When [Jesus] saw the crowds, he felt compassion for them, because they were distressed and dejected, like sheep without a shepherd." The King of the universe looked on his special creation, on humans, and saw that they were helpless. And he decided to do something about it.

He left his palace in heaven, and he went to war. He didn't send armies out to fight Satan. He didn't position angel hosts to defy the armies of hell. He himself led the charge, alone and unarmed.

Jesus crushed the dark lord when he sacrificed himself on the cross. And he showed himself the victor when, amazingly, he rose from the dead. This was an epic battle, an epic struggle, a quest. Jesus set out to regain what he had lost.

He set out to find *you*.

That's right. In this true quest, you are not the hero.

You are the one who has been rescued.

Or the World Falls

"But I don't want to be rescued!" you say. "I want to be Frodo!" If Frodo doesn't get the ring to Mount Doom, the world falls to the power of Sauron. The world needs Frodo.

Yeah, I get it. I'd rather be the hero, too. I am the hero in my daydreams!

You are not Frodo, though.

Remember: The Big Quest of rescuing the world is done. If you fail, or if you seem to fail, the world does not fall into darkness because of you. Jesus already did the work. Jesus already died. Jesus already rose again. Your actions, no matter how much you think you bungle them, cannot thwart God's plans.

But in the weird way that God works... that doesn't mean you're useless, either. You're not a mere prop that's been rescued and now sits around looking pretty. (Which is a really good thing for those of us who aren't that pretty.) You are still important in this true story. He still has things for you to do.

Yeah, I can't quite wrap my mind around it either.

But you are so important that Jesus left heaven to rescue you. And then, he made you part of something bigger. He gave you a quest.

He's put you in a massive fellowship. There aren't any elves or dwarves in this fellowship (that I know of), but there's a lot of weirdos. People like you and me, bound together in the same quest, working together to proclaim the truth: The war's been won! Jesus defeated darkness!

See, Jesus didn't just rescue you. He came in and saved the entire world... but the world doesn't know it. So he sends the Holy Spirit to bring life to dead people, one by one. Ephesians 2:1-5 says it this way: "And you were dead in your trespasses and sins in which you previously lived according to the ways of this world, according to the ruler of the power of the air, the spirit now working in the disobedient. We too all previously lived among them in our fleshly desires, carrying out the inclinations of our flesh and thoughts, and we were by nature children under wrath as the others were also. But God, who is rich in mercy, because of his great love that he had for us, made us alive with Christ even though we were dead in trespasses. You are saved by grace!"

You were dead. Jesus made you alive.

And he put you in a fellowship to do something new: Wake up the rest of the world. Show them. Tell them. The Hero has come and rescued you.

Your Quest

You want a quest? You want a purpose? Here it is. This matters. What you do here will echo forever. It won't just be a story.

Jesus made you part of something bigger. He gave you a quest.

Think about what Jesus said. One day, he's looking out over some grain fields that are just waiting to be harvested. And it reminds him of all the people that need to be told of the victory that at that point he was about to win. And he says, "Therefore, pray to the Lord of the harvest to send out workers into his harvest" (Luke 10:2). Jesus says, "Ask God to send people out to join this quest!"

And the very next thing he says? "Now go; I'm sending you out like lambs among wolves" (Luke 10:3).

You. You are part of this quest. A quest to go and tell what Jesus has done. Your role will not be easy; you're surrounded by wolves. But you have a purpose, and that purpose reaches into eternity. And no matter how you fail, because Jesus carried your burdens to the cross, on the last day Jesus will look at you and say, "Well done, good and faithful servant." Well done.

You will have completed the quest.

Your Lord smiles on you.

And can you imagine, ten thousand years from now, in heaven, a person walks up to you and embraces you. "Because of you, I'm here! Because of you, I got to know our Lord!"

You try to figure out who this person is. You've never seen him before!

"You told my great-great-grandfather about Jesus. And God used those seeds you planted to create faith. And he told his children, and they told their children – because of you, generations of us are here now!"

And the two of you sing to your Lord about how good he is.

Using Quests to Share Jesus

Think about saying this to someone:

"I hate feeling useless. Like, I get that when I work, I'm doing something that helps... somewhere. But I wish that what I did *mattered*, don't you?

Can you imagine if maybe it did matter? What would that be like?

What if I told you we really are part of something epic? Like, changing the world? Not that I'm changing the world, but I'm part of something that did change the world and continues to change the world? Well, I guess I have to tell you, it didn't start with me. Actually, I was trapped. You ever feel trapped? Yeah, me too. But I was rescued! And the man who rescued me, well, his name is Jesus. He still does some pretty amazing things... and he takes me along for the ride!"

> *What if I told you we really are part of something epic?*

Are You Pondering What I'm Pondering?

The next time you encounter a story with a quest, ask:

- ✓ What is the goal of the quest? How does that quest provide a reflection of the quest God has given me?

- ✓ What will happen if the characters fail the quest? What happens if I fail my quest?

- ✓ What was Jesus's quest? What would happen if he failed his quest?

- ✓ What difficulties do the characters encounter in their quest? What difficulties do I encounter in my quest?

The next time you find yourself enjoying a story with a quest, ask:

- ✓ What elements of this quest do I most enjoy? What attracts me to them?

- ✓ As I enjoy this story, do I feel a desire to have a quest like that? What makes this particular quest more attractive to me than the quest God has given?

- ✓ Did I enjoy the *ending* of the story's quest? How is that a reflection of the end of my quest, when that comes?

- ✓ How single-minded were the characters in the quest? How single-minded am I in pursuing my quest?

Meditations on Quests

The Quest of the Son of God

So often in stories with quests, the main character either is royalty or becomes royalty. They fight to save a kingdom that's their own from the beginning, or the kingdom they fight to save becomes theirs.

Jesus was already Prince of the universe, but he chose to go questing anyway. His quest was a little different, though. It was to save a kingdom that had rebelled against him.

In other words... Jesus fought to rescue the bad guys. He fought to save us. We said he was our Lord, but did we listen? No. We put up other kings to rule our lives. Kings like, "I need their approval" or "I need to feel good in *this* way." Kings that really didn't help us. Kings that turned on us and turned out to not be nearly as good as we thought they'd be.

We were lost. We had rejected a good King and chased after worthless kings.

> *In other words...*
> *Jesus fought to*
> *rescue the bad guys.*

But Jesus came to seek and to save what was lost (Luke 19:10). That was his quest.

Now, imagine the determination of characters that go on quests. They will accomplish the task, no matter what! But usually at some point of the story they give up. Maybe they wander. Maybe they get lost, and they're not sure how to go forward.

Not Jesus. He knew his goal: Rescue the lost. And he knew how to achieve that goal: Die for them, and then rise from the dead. So that's exactly what he did.

Nothing got between Jesus and his quest. Many tried. Some people offered him fame. Some offered him comfort. Everything you could think of tried to get between Jesus and his quest.

He never fell for a single temptation.

And when it came time to complete the quest, Jesus didn't blink. Yes, you might remember he asked: If there's any other way, let's do that. But... not what I will, but what you will, Father. And then Jesus went forward to the cross because that was the completion of his quest. That's what it took to rescue the lost.

This is the God you worship: the God who had a quest to rescue you. And he succeeded in his quest. And now that he's succeeded, he rejoices to have you as his own. Hebrews 12:2 says, "For the joy that lay before him, [Jesus] endured the cross." For the joy of winning you.

His quest was arduous. It brought pain. But it was worth it to him.

And now, the Quest is over. Jesus won.

Prayer: Dear Jesus, thank you for pursuing your quest to rescue me. Thank you for succeeding. I praise you for making me your own! Amen.

---

*And now, the Quest
is over. Jesus won.*

The Quest of the Children of God

In many stories with quests, there is a commissioning scene. Maybe the main characters already want to go on on this journey, but now someone says, "This is something you must do." I think of the scene in *The Fellowship of the Ring* when Frodo reaches for the One Ring and says he will go on this quest, and he is then sent out with a, well, fellowship to take the Ring to Mount Doom. That scene is pivotal; it means that the characters are acting on behalf of others – maybe just the king, maybe for entire nations.

> *You have been sent out to rescue other lost people.*

Can you imagine what that might feel like? To know that you have been sent out by someone who knows you have it in you, that you are the best hope to achieve this goal, that you are commissioned and acting on behalf of something bigger than yourself?

Well, you don't have to imagine. You've been commissioned. Maybe you've even heard of it: The Great Commission.

In Matthew 28:18-20, Jesus says, "All authority has been given to me in heaven and on earth. Go, therefore, and make disciples of all nations, baptizing them in the name of the Father and of the Son and of the Holy Spirit, teaching them to observe everything I have commanded you. And remember, I am with you always, to the end of the age."

That's a pretty big quest. You have been sent out to rescue other lost people. You have been sent out not just by a king, but by the King of kings. And he has full confidence in your abilities, because he's the same one who gave you those abilities in the first place!

You've been sent out on a mission of rescue. Not to show that you're better than anyone else. Not to teach people how to behave. Your quest is to point to Jesus, who already paid to rescue them.

And you've failed in that quest, haven't you?

In *The Fellowship of the Ring*, Boromir rejects the quest and seeks to use the Ring for his own ends. He fails, and suffers for it. How about you? How many times have you rejected your quest? I know I have, so many times. I get scared of what other people will think or what the consequences will be if I actually pursue this quest.

When that happens, go back to Jesus's quest: He came to seek and to save the lost.

To save you.

He knew how many times you would fail... and he still doesn't regret rescuing you. He doesn't regret paying that price.

Jesus succeeded in his quest. And now he goes with you on yours, to the end of the age. Now you go and pursue your quest.

Prayer: Jesus, you completed your quest, and that is my hope. Now you have commissioned me to go and show people how you have rescued them. Forgive me for the times I've rejected that quest. Instead, remind me of your power, and strengthen me to pursue the quest you've given me to the end of my life. Amen.

The Quest Fails

When Boromir failed in pursuing the quest at the end of *The Fellowship of the Ring*, he paid a heavy price: he died. (Though he did die heroically!) If he had succeeded in derailing the quest, all of Middle-earth would have fallen to darkness.

In stories, when people fail in their quests, the consequences are dire. Nations fall. Worlds end. People die.

Jesus had a quest: Seek and save the lost. He succeeded.

You have a quest: Seek and save the lost. Show them Jesus.

What happens when you fail?

It would be easy to panic here. "If I don't pursue my quest, people go to hell! I'm responsible for the souls of so many people around me!" And then we start stressing out and hyper-ventilating. Panic attack! We don't act very heroic then, do we?

When that happens... go look at the guy who completed his quest. What does King Jesus say? "This is the will of him who sent me: that I should lose none of those he has given me but should raise them up on the last day" (John 6:39).

Did you catch that?

Jesus not only won in his quest to redeem the world... he knows everyone he has saved, and he will save them.

He graciously invites you into this quest. He wants to bring you into his fellowship of saving others! But if you fail, don't despair. Jesus already knows whom he's rescued, and he will save them one way or another. Maybe someone else will connect them to Jesus. Maybe someone else will remind them of what they once knew.

> *You have a quest: Seek and save the lost. Show them Jesus. What happens if you fail?*

So, don't worry. Yes, pursue your quest. But if you fail, worlds will not end because of your actions. Jesus will not lose a single person who belongs to him. And you've already got Jesus's victory, too. Now go stand in his victory, confident that even when you fail, because Jesus won, you win too.

Prayer: Jesus, so often I've failed. Help me to remember that you already won the victory. Give me confidence in what you've already given me, and give me the courage, wisdom, and opportunity to share it. Amen.

Trope Seven

Cannon Fodder

"JUST ONCE, I'D LIKE TO MAKE IT TO THE END CREDITS."

Trope 7: Cannon Fodder

The End of the Quest

"It'll kill them. It'll kill all of them." I trembled as I read the faded ink on the scroll I held.

"Do it, Salaya!!" Aramath bellowed at me from the door. He muttered, releasing another spell down the stairs. The orb of light hurtled past Bayana, Devin, and Shuran, the last of our companions.

The last of them the orcs hadn't slaughtered.

The tower trembled. The orcs were trampling through our magical defenses by sheer numbers. Soon they'd be here.

Soon they'd kill these friends, too.

I read through the scroll again, remembering the runes, all the things I'd been taught. I translated the spell into my own language. Like putting together a good dough, the right ingredients gathered in my mind and I combined them. The power charged my arms, my fingertips. One part sorrow, two parts rage. Mix until ready to froth over.

The baby cried.

The orphaned orc Shuran had taken in on our journey. She lay in the corner of the tower room, kicking her tiny legs.

All of them. My father's spell would kill anyone with orc blood. It would end the war, just like that. It would save the human lands. The elven kingdoms would at last be avenged.

And that baby would die, too.

And the children we'd met. The half-bloods. It wasn't their fault who they were.

Leave the spell to rise. When the power has doubled in size, release it.

The spell grew inside me. The ingredients were mixed. The dough was proving inside my heart. One part sorrow, two parts rage. All the runes flavoring the mix.

Screaming and the sound of blades striking against each other sounded from the hall.

"Salaya!" Aramath bellowed again. "Release the spell! Quickly! We can't hold them for long!"

Kill every orc. Destroy an entire race, innocent and guilty.

Or watch my friends die.

I shut my eyes and prayed.

A Rather Murderous Trope

After all, they're faceless minions that exist only to be wiped out.

The bad guy has all sorts of people working for him. Maybe they're orcs. Maybe they're stormtroopers. Maybe they're just faceless goons. It doesn't really matter what they are; for the most part, they only exist to get beaten up by the good guys. They're cannon fodder. Everyone else seems to fear them, but the main characters? They can eat these guys for breakfast.

Well, not literally.

But they do kill quite a few of them – maybe they even get into a competition to see who can kill more! After all, they're faceless minions that exist only to be wiped out.

In Real Life, There Are No Minions

We have a problem. We have these stunning main characters. They're amazing, but how do we get that across? How do we show how powerful they are?

Oh, I know! Let's build up that the bad guy has an army that terrifies everyone. Stormtroopers that never miss! Orcs that all the lands fear! The bigger and the uglier the faceless mass of bad guys, the better. Show their prowess!

And then... just have the heroes mow them down. Stormtroopers fall by the score. Orcs lie slain on the ground. And your heroes did it!

They might even crack a few jokes about it!

Yep, if you want to show how amazing your heroes are, have them take on armies of faceless minions.

Yes! Feel like a Klingon! Drink from the skulls of your enemies!

It feels good, doesn't it? You get a little aggression out this way. I gotta tell you, there's little that gets me as excited as watching the Rohirrim ride forth in *The Two Towers* or Luke Skywalker take on Jabba's goons in *Return of the Jedi*. There's a little bit of vicarious living going on, isn't there? If the hero can stand tall over their enemies, maybe we can, too.

Yes! Feel like a Klingon! Drink from the skulls of your enemies!

But in real life... there are no faceless minions.

Things sort of shift when you think: Those stormtroopers, if they're people... they have souls. How many of those orcs marched in the military to support their families back home? What if all those bad guys have children that will cry when daddy doesn't come home?

But in real life... there are no faceless minions.

Suddenly all that cheering for the deaths of our enemies feels really sadistic, doesn't it?

When I was young, 80's cartoon shows often employed soulless robots as the bad guys. I remember Leonardo of the *Teenage Mutant Ninja Turtles* slicing through countless Foot Clan ninjas that were robots. You could take out all the bad guys without feeling bad for them! It changed the formula just enough: Make the good guys look good by having them wipe out a legion of beings that didn't have anyone back home worrying about them.

But what about a lot of geek fiction now? Some might still use robots (Do Cybermen count? Borg?), but generally they use living, thinking beings.

There are no small parts.

The reason we can enjoy the mass destruction of so many enemies is that they're faceless. We don't know anything about them except that they're bad guys. Who's that? It's an orc. He must be bad. And just so we don't confuse anyone, let's make sure he's really ugly, and maybe he's hungry enough to eat the main character. If all we know about a character consists of bad things, we don't mind so much when they get taken out by an elven arrow.

In a fantasy world where you make the rules, you can do that. We can say that in this story, the orcs really are just mindless killing machines.

But in real life it doesn't work that way.

In real life, every person you encounter (and every person you don't encounter) matters. Every single person has a real life. They aren't mindless stormtroopers. They have worth.

You are not an extra off to the side when it comes to Jesus. You are prized.

How do I know?

Because I trust Jesus. Listen to what it says in 1 Peter 1:18-19: "For you know that you were redeemed from your empty way of life inherited from your fathers, not with perishable things like silver or gold, but with the precious blood of Christ, like that of an unblemished and spotless lamb."

Jesus looked at you and said, "You're worth this much to me: my own blood." He examined you. He knew you inside and out. And he said, "I'll pay this price. I'll pay my own life to buy you back from sin, death, and Satan himself. You are mine now!"

You are valued so, so much. You are not an extra off to the side when it comes to Jesus. You are prized.

And he paid the same amount for that person who eats lunch over there that you've never talked to. And he paid just as much for the person who voted for the other guy in the last election. And he paid that dear, dear price for the person in another nation who wants to see this nation fall.

> There is no "faceless enemy" for Jesus. Jesus cares enough to die for them.

In other words, there is no "faceless enemy" for Jesus. Instead of wading through the hordes of his enemies, Jesus cares enough to die for them.

Yeah. I said enemies.

Romans 8:7 says, "The mind-set of the flesh is hostile to God." See, until Jesus chose us, we weren't just random extras wandering around the background. We were actually part of those endless orc armies. We were the bad guys.

Jesus changed that. 2 Corinthians 5:17 says, "Therefore, if anyone is in Christ, the new creation has come: The old has gone, the new is here!" You don't belong to the orc armies anymore. You belong in the good guy army. And even there, you're not an extra.

You were hand-chosen and paid for.

And so is the guy who made your sandwich for lunch. And so is the woman sitting two cars behind you at the stoplight. And so is the person who put the makeup on Klingon #4. Jesus paid for them.

They're not mindless extras. They're not stormtroopers for us to mow down.

They are ones who Jesus died for.

So that means we can't fight armies of goons, right?

What am I saying here? That movies that portray the heroes taking down armies of bad guys should be avoided? That novels that show off the skills of the protagonists against faceless antagonists are evil? That any fiction that includes armies is wrong?

Nope.

God gave a command in Exodus 20:13: "You shall not murder." That sounds pretty cut-and-dry, right? Let's not kill the orcs. Don't shoot back at the stormtroopers. Just be nice to them.

Wait a second!

God gave us the gift of life, and he wants us to not just "not murder." He wants us to defend life! That means that if some Klingon comes at you with a bat'leth, you don't have to take it in your chest without fighting back. Defend your own life! God gave that life, too! Remember, you're not an extra. Jesus paid for you. That means you have worth! Defend what God has given!

> *We are also called to protect the lives of others – not just our own lives.*

Sure, we don't get to just go out and mow down all the Klingons with our advanced lightsabers. But we defend and protect.

And yes. We are also called to protect the lives of others – not just our own lives.

What that means is that yes, it's OK to serve in the military. At least in theory, the military exists to protect the people of the nation.

And what that means for stories like *The Lord of the Rings* is, when Aragorn leads his people out against the orcs of Mordor, he's not doing it because he hates orcs. He's doing it to protect the people of Middle-earth. He is acting as a guard, stepping between defenseless people and a terrible enemy.

That doesn't mean the "other side" is mindless minions. It means that the people behind you need protecting, and that job falls to the heroes.

So, watch your stories. If the heroes are taking out the bad guys and laughing about it, maybe keep in mind that in the real world, there are no mindless enemies that you can mow down. Every soul is precious. If the good guys hunt down enemies that are not threats, keep in mind that we are called to protect, not get revenge. Be discerning as you take in these stories.

Using Armies of Orcs to Share Jesus

Did you ever feel like you were just an extra in a story? Like the main character was over there, and you didn't matter. Or worse, you were on the wrong side, and the hero was going to come and take you out at any moment? Maybe you've been the faceless girl in the crowd at school or the odd man out at work. No one seemed to care about you, unless of course you could take the blame for them. Unless the boss was looking for someone to cut.

Yeah. It's so easy to feel unimportant, isn't it? Other people sometimes treat us like "Random Dude #17" in the background and trample right past us intent on being the hero. We're expendable to them.

But you're not just a throw-away movie extra. You're not a carbon-copy stormtrooper.

But you're not just a throw-away movie extra. You're not a carbon-copy stormtrooper. Did you know that God looked over the entire world, and he saw you? And he saw everything you've ever done. He saw everything you ever thought. And yeah, you were on the wrong side.

But the Hero came to rescue you.

Yeah! Jesus chose you! He chose to save you. And he didn't pay with gold or silver. He paid with his own blood. Here, let me tell you about it...

Are You Pondering What I'm Pondering?

The next time you encounter a story that involves lots of killing of faceless bad guys, ask:

- ✓ Why are the heroes fighting all these bad guys?
- ✓ What attitude do the heroes have toward having to kill these bad guys?
- ✓ Are the bad guys being treated as people, or merely something "in the way" of the heroes?
- ✓ What cause are the heroes fighting for? What price are they willing to pay to achieve their goal?

The next time you enjoy a story that involves the killing of faceless bad guys, ask:

- ✓ Why am I enjoying this particular scene?
- ✓ Do I treat the people around me as faceless extras or people that Jesus cared enough to die for?
- ✓ How can I protect the people around me?
- ✓ How would this scene be different if the heroes treated the bad guys as people? Would I enjoy it as much, even if the heroes still had to fight to defend themselves?

Meditations on the Killing of Orcs

The Death of the Wicked

I can't wait to see the Avengers take out the invading army of bad guys. Or Gimli and Legolas fight to see who can kill the most orcs. Or to find out if the X-Wings will destroy more TIE-Fighters. That's what I want to happen to the bad guys! Show me some cool moves; show me some awesome action, and make sure the bad guys are hurting when it's done!

But God wants something vastly different. Ezekiel 33:11 says, "Tell them, 'As I live—this is the declaration of the Lord God—I take no pleasure in the death of the wicked, but rather that the wicked person should turn from his way and live. Repent, repent of your evil ways!'"

> God doesn't want to see a great action scene where they're all finally taken out.

Did you catch that? God doesn't want evil people to pay for their sins. He doesn't want to see a great action scene where they're all finally taken out.

He would rather show mercy. He longs to forgive.

I said before that I want to make sure the bad guys are hurting when it's done. What would happen if I got my way?

Well, if God is the one defining evil (and he's probably the best person to do it), that means that every sin is evil. Every time I have failed to love those around me. Every time I have thought of my comfort first. Every time I have ignored what God commands, I am the one who should be wiped out.

But God wanted me to turn from my sin. He's the one who came and took my punishment from me. He's the one who declared me holy. He's the one who chose me.

God wanted to have mercy on me, and he paid the price to make sure it could happen.

It means that God will not take me out. I'm not a part of the bad guys anymore. I belong to him. And so do you!

And God desires that everyone that still doesn't know him would turn to him. He doesn't want to wipe out the bad guy army... He wants them to join his side.

And God has a good way to go about it. Instead of cheering on our destruction, God changes us.

Let's be a part of that process, too. Let's keep from desiring the death of the wicked. Let's pray that they turn from their ways and live.

And watch out. Because God will use you to tell them about the God who loved them even when they were enemies... just like he loved you.

Prayer: Lord, thank you for not desiring my death but turning me from my wicked ways. Help me to see the people around me as people you died for. Help me to desire what's best for them, too. Amen.

No Violence Shall Touch My Hands

In *The Wheel of Time* by Robert Jordan, the Tuatha'an are a people that abhor all violence. They won't even defend themselves when attacked.

Are they right? After all, aren't Christians supposed to love their neighbors, not attack them?

Well, if all violence is wrong, Jesus sinned. In John 2, Jesus sees that people have turned the Temple into a place to sell things. There's so much distraction from worshiping God, Jesus gets angry. He makes a whip and flips over tables and drives people out of the Temple.

> *Well, if all violence is wrong, Jesus sinned.*

These are not the actions of a man who refuses to commit any violence!

What's going on? Well, Jesus sees that this marketplace that's been set up is keeping people from worshiping God. Jesus is angry that anything would ever come between God and his people. Imagine how angry you would be if you saw someone come between a child and her parent! And Jesus acts to protect the people and allow them to worship.

In Luke 3:14, John the Baptist is approached by some soldiers who ask, "'What should we do?' [John] said to them, 'Don't take money from anyone by force or false accusation, and be satisfied with your wages.'"

John didn't tell the soldiers to stop being soldiers. He didn't tell them to not employ violence. You might think John was just being nice, but this is John the Baptist we're talking about. He called people "A brood of vipers." Look, you don't call people that unless you're not afraid of upsetting them.

Instead of telling the soldiers to stop being violent, John told them to not abuse their role as soldiers. Don't use violence or the threat of violence to get your way. Be satisfied with what you get.

Does that mean I think all violence is good?

No.

Let me make this really clear: To intentionally harm another is a sin. Period.

But to step in to *prevent* violence, to protect another, to stand up and say, "You will not harm them!" – that is what we should do.

And for any violence you have done, and for any violence you have wanted to do but didn't only because you didn't want to get caught or hurt yourself, if you have longed to harm someone that God loves dearly and that Jesus died for, know this: "He was assigned a grave with the wicked, but he was with a rich man at his death, because he had done no violence and had not spoken deceitfully" (Isaiah 53:9).

Jesus knew when it was sinful to commit violence and when it was done in protection of others. And there was no confusion in him.

And because he is your substitute, you have his record.

Do not fear: You have been rescued from the violence you have done.

Prayer: Jesus, forgive me for the violence I have done and for the times I have not stood up to protect. Thank you for giving me your record. Help me to stand up to protect others, while remembering your love for all people. Amen.

Not an Expendable Extra

My favorite character in *Return of the Jedi* is Stormtrooper #27. He's one of the guys standing in the landing bay of the Death Star when the Emperor arrives. You know which one I'm talking about, right?

No?

Well, I'm not terribly surprised. I mean, it's not like he's a fan favorite. Or that anyone knows anything about him, except whatever extra filled in the costume for that day of filming.

That particular scene has all the stormtroopers. There's nothing we know about them except they work for the Empire. And really, when the Death Star blows up and everyone celebrates... does anyone in the movie even think about all the stormtroopers that just died?

Do you ever feel like Stormtrooper #27? Like you're just an extra in life? That if you disappeared, most people wouldn't blink?

It's my guess that most of the "big people" making the movie didn't know or care about Stormtrooper #27. They probably didn't know his name. Why bother? He's not important.

But someone way more important than an actor or movie director knows your name.

Isaiah 43:1 says, "Now this is what the Lord says... 'Do not fear, for I have redeemed you; I have called you by your name; you are mine.'"

> **Do you ever feel like Stormtrooper #27?**

God calls you *by name*. He looks through all the ages of humanity, he looks through the billions of people on the planet, and you don't fade into the background to him. He knows you by name.

And he doesn't know you by name because you mess up all the time. He doesn't roll his eyes when he thinks about you. He doesn't sigh and say, "Oh, yeah, *her*."

He has redeemed you. That's why he knows who you are. He has chosen to pay the price for you to be his very own.

And he knows more about you than just your name. Matthew 10:30 says, "But even the hairs of your head have all been counted."

Have you ever played *Dungeons and Dragons* or any other tabletop role playing game? In most of those games, you fill out a character sheet. You write down whatever's important. I know a lot of people that skip the physical description stuff and just get to the statistics: strength, dexterity, and so on.

But Jesus didn't skip anything for you, and what he knows about you is way more detailed than any character sheet. He even knows how many hairs are on your head right now and how many you'll have there a week from now. He knows everything about you.

And he still loves you.

You are no extra. You are a chosen child of God, who is pleased to have you as his own.

Prayer: Lord, thank you for noticing me, for making me your own, for saying that I am special to you. That blows me away. Move me to celebrate that you claim me as your child always. Amen.

Trope Eight

Dashing Rogues

"WOW, HE'S REALLY LET HIMSELF GO."

Trope 8: Dashing Rogues

Always Have a Backup Plan

It's never a good idea to steal from an orc. I probably should have known that already, though.

Right now, the orc was shoving my face into the dirt floor of one of the huts of the village. His rank breath washed over me. "Where is it, human? My idol. Give it back."

"Which one?" I tried smiling.

Ever tried smiling while an orc is in the process of crushing your skull? It's not the easiest thing in the world at all. I had learned how to smile through all sorts of pain, of course. Won't bore you with that list right now, but I'd gotten myself into all sorts of situations in the last sixteen years, which is coincidentally how hold I am. I can say this much, though: I never got into the same trouble twice.

Usually.

"The idol you stole from me," the orc said back, enunciating each word through his twisted mouth.

"I'm sorry to say, but I need to ask again: Which one? I've stolen a lot of household idols today."

Ah. Apparently, that was the wrong thing to say. How much pressure could a human skull take before it's completely crushed?

Well, apparently a little bit more. I have a very thick skull, it turns out.

Ow.

The orc screamed some gibberish. Something about ancestors and honor and all that rot. I wasn't really paying a lot of attention at that moment, what with the skull and all that. And the smell. Smells can be pretty distracting too, you know.

The orc caught the smell, too. "What smells like megaphant piss?"

"Probably me," I grunted through the pain. "I just broke a vial of it. See, you never tied my hands, and I've got several vials in my belt."

The orc finally stood up from the ground and backed away quickly. "They'll smell it!"

"That was the plan," I smiled. "Always good to have a backup. My first plans never seem to go well." I struggled up from the floor as the ground trembled. "Wow, they really do have a good sense of smell, don't they?"

The orc ran to the door right as the entire wall of the hut burst and the megaphant stampeded through.

And that's when I realized that my backup really wasn't a great plan. Sure, getting the megaphant to charge would get the orc away from me. But how was I going to get away from something that even orcs fear?

A Dashing Trope

They break all the rules, and they look good while they do it.

They break all the rules, and they look good while they do it. The dashing rogue often is in it for themselves at the start of the story, just trying to get ahead. They're often in trouble with authority in one way or another. They might fire first just to make sure they win, especially if their life is on the line. While they might be good in a fight, they're more likely to use their wits (or try to use their wits) to get out of trouble.

Think Han Solo. Think Flynn Rider from *Tangled*. Think about almost all the main characters in *The Princess Bride*. Think the crew from *Firefly*.

They're the cool kids. They're the dashing rogues.

Bad Boys are Cool, Right?

Let's face it: the rogues are the awesome ones. They sit in the corners of their taverns, watching everyone come and go. They know they're in danger, but they act like they don't care. And yes, I already said it, but: They shoot first.

> *The rogues are the awesome ones... Oh, and they usually get the girl, too.*

But I want to ask: What is it that makes them so cool? What is this aura around a well-written rogue that instantly attracts us to them?

There are a number of reasons. One is their utter confidence. We see that they know what they're doing. They have plans and backup plans. Even if they get someone angry, they always seem to have one last friend that can get them out of a scrape. And through it all, if someone calls them crummy or stuck-up or a nerf herder, well, it doesn't bother them.

At least, not much.

Oh, and they usually get the girl, too. (I find it interesting that most of the rogues I can think of are men. While there are certainly women rogues, they seem far fewer in number.)

What fills a rogue with such confidence? Why is it they face every situation with a smile and a clever barb?

They know they're just that good. They've honed their skills in various crucibles. They've used their skills to overcome, or at least survive, impossible odds, time and time again. So, when another challenge comes their way, they can laugh.

Or fake a laugh.

One of the interesting things about many rogues is that when we get to know their personalities, they're relatively frail. Han Solo ends up coming back to save Luke. Inigo Montoya is really searching for the man who killed his father.

But they cover up their weakness quickly with another quip.

"I love you."

"I know."

Once again: One of the reasons we love rogues is that they're so confident. And the thing they're confident in is themselves.

A Reason for Confidence

Do you wish you could have that kind of confidence? That swagger? The brain for those kinds of quips and the ability to shoot a blaster or handle a rapier like a rogue?

I'd like to think I'm full of quips, but my children would probably disagree.

Well, I did take a couple years in fencing, and let me tell you, it's a lot of fun (and work). And I'd like to think I'm full of quips, but my children would probably disagree with that assessment. And swagger is a learned thing. You can learn a lot. Maybe you could learn all those skills.

But whether you can handle a sword or find yourself tongue-tied every time you face someone as intimidating as a rabbit with big sharp pointy teeth, you have a huge reason for confidence. And that confidence is not based in you.

See, if you're Christian, you know something that's incredibly demoralizing: You're not really all that strong.

Yeah. I'm sorry, but it's true.

In my congregation, we actually say about the same thing just about every Sunday right at the beginning of our weekly worship services: I confess that I am a sinner.

Me.

When I look in the mirror, I see someone who has failed so many, many times. When I'm honest, I see that I have no reason for confidence in any of my skills, any of my talents, any of, well, me.

And I don't even have to be a Christian to see that. We've all been failed by our talents. We've depended on them, and they've fritzed out at the wrong moment. I know my skills never seem to hold up when I need them. And let's face it: I've messed up things for me so often, if I swagger, well, it's all faked. Or it should be, at least, if I'm honest.

That doesn't sound very rogue-like though, does it?

Well, honestly, it's not. Rogues can give the smolder because they're convinced they're *all that*, and Christians know we're not.

But we have a much, much better reason for confidence.

Self-confidence focuses on *my* ability to do what needs to be done. Except I have no reason to have that kind of confidence.

But if I'm confident in Jesus? If I'm confident in *his* ability to do what needs to be done?

> *But then God planned the perfect heist. He was going to steal you back.*

OK, sure. I know that Jesus can do anything. Sure, he's God. We got that covered. But let's be honest, shall we? Jesus doesn't exactly swing this world my way too often. Not the way I like it.

But then we get to the catch: If Jesus doesn't swing the world my way, it's because his way is better.

Have you ever seen *Ocean's Eleven*? Yeah, yeah, that's not a science fiction or fantasy movie, but go with me here for a moment. It's a heist movie filled with cunning rogues. They're trying to steal a bunch of money from a casino. In the end, it looks like they've lost.

But then at the end, you find the twist: They knew what they were doing all along. The audience finally gets to see all the things we didn't see before as they prepared for the heist, and we get to say, "Ah!"

God is kind of like that kind of rogue.

He's got a plan. He's got a heist going on. And what he's stealing is you. You were hanging in the Devil's gallery. He cackled over you. He loved that you belonged to him!

But then God planned the perfect heist. He was going to steal you back. And he snuck right in. The Devil thought he was winning. He thought he'd caught Jesus red-handed. He thought that his security system had stopped him. The Devil didn't even bother calling the cops; he just had Jesus killed.

Ah.

But that's the twist: The very act of Jesus dying freed us from the Devil's grasp. He had it planned from the beginning.

Yep. I just called Jesus a clever rogue. And it's easy to do that, because he's the one who always should have had perfect confidence in himself. He had perfect timing, perfect skills, perfect talent. And instead of using it to make himself rich or get the girl, he used it to get *you*.

And if his planning is that good, if he can handle that kind of twist, and if he did it all to get you... do you really think he's going to let anything happen to you that doesn't fit into his master plan?

That Savior Swagger

So, what does that mean for you and your lovable rogues?

Well, it means that you can be just as confident as them, but again, not in your skills. You can face whatever you face, knowing it will work out for your best. There's a rogue on your side, and his master plan is so much better than anything you can put together.

That does take balance to pull off: to be confident and not a jerk.

Of course, that doesn't mean that you're always going to be smiling. In Jesus's master plan, he's going to get you home safe and sound to heaven, but there will be all sorts of twists and turns along the way.

We love rogues because whatever other people say doesn't seem to bother them.

You? Guess what? If you know that the master plan is being acted out right now, that you've already got your place safe in heaven, and that the master thief not only risked everything but gave everything to rescue you, well, who cares what they think?

Now, that doesn't mean you should be an overconfident jerk. If you're sneaking into a tower and some young woman is going to whack you with a frying pan, that doesn't mean you show her the smolder. Maybe you apologize for sneaking into her home and run away. Or offer to take her to see some lanterns, if you think she's being held against her will by her mother.

That does take balance to pull off: to be confident and not a jerk. And if you pull it off, if your confidence is in Jesus and not in you, I think you can find that balance. After all, you're not confident in your abilities. You're just confident in Jesus.

And if you end up looking a bit like a rogue, well, that's not so bad, is it?

Using Rogues to Share Jesus

Did you know that there are some dashing rogues in the Bible?

Yeah. Seriously.

See, these rogues were all very assured... but they were all sinful.

You ever hear of a guy named Samson? Now there's a guy with swagger. If we're talking fantasy tropes, you might think he's more of a barbarian, but even barbarians can be rogues. Just talk to Conan. Samson was clever, and he had a confidence that was insane. Read some of his stories from Judges 13-16.

How about a guy named Ehud? We don't know much about him, except he was sneaky and clever. And he had some guts. He was left-handed and underestimated. Israel was under the thumb of an invading king. Ehud delivered some tax money to this king, a guy by the name of Eglon, who could well have been a body double for Jabba the Hutt. Ehud strapped a sword to his inner thigh; apparently the guards didn't bother searching him. After all, he was some left-handed underdog. And then Ehud told Eglon he had a secret message. Eglon fell for it and sent the guards away. And then Ehud killed the evil king, like you do. Check out his story in Judges 3:15-30.

Then there's some guys that snuck into a city to check out its defenses. They ended up visiting a prostitute's house, but this prostitute had a heart of gold (speaking of tropes...). She concealed them and helped them escape. Joshua 2 tells their story.

And David. Oh, man, David. He took out a giant with a sling. He became something of a bandit king, quite against his will, but read his story with Nabal. It's in I Samuel 25. Go ahead check it out; that's not a story you usually get in Sunday school. Tell me that doesn't make you think of a dashing rogue.

So, what does all this have to do with sharing Jesus?

Well, if you read these guys' stories, you'll see that they're all incredibly... human. They're sinful.

Samson was an egotistical jerk that ignored everything God said and chased after women.

Samson was an egotistical jerk that ignored everything God said and chased after women. Ehud sure did his best to save Israel, but it all fell apart rather quickly. Those two spies in Jericho? What were they doing visiting a prostitute's house? (We're not told one way or another, but you have to admit, it is a bit suspicious.) And David. Ah, David. He knew sin very well.

See, these rogues were all very assured... but they were all sinful. They all failed. But look what happened anyway: they were forgiven because they trusted that a Savior would come for them.

In other words, you can use rogues to share Jesus by telling these rogues' stories and showing how they were sinful, too. And you can show how they trusted someone to come and forgive their sins.

Tell any story from the Bible correctly, and eventually you'll discover you're telling Jesus's story.

And if you're doing that, well, you're sharing Jesus.

Are You Pondering What I'm Pondering?

The next time you encounter a story with a dashing rogue, ask these questions:

- ✓ Why does this dashing rogue act the way he does?
- ✓ What causes him or her to have such confidence?
- ✓ Does that confidence have a good basis in reality?
- ✓ Does this rogue ever show that he or she is actually not as self-assured as they appear?

The next time you enjoy a story that employs a dashing rogue, ask these questions:

- ✓ What about the dashing rogue do I find most interesting?
- ✓ Do I wish I had that kind of confidence?
- ✓ Why don't I have that kind of confidence?
- ✓ If Jesus really has stolen me in the greatest heist ever, what kind of confidence can I have?

Tell any story from the Bible correctly, and eventually you'll discover you're telling Jesus's story.

Meditations on Dashing Rogues

We Like Bad Boys

Maybe you don't like dashing rogues because of their silver tongues, quick blades, and utter confidence in themselves. Maybe you like them because they're the bad boys. They laugh at the rules and do their own thing.

> We all hate rules. They're always in the way.

And there's a certain kind of attraction there, isn't there? We all hate rules. They're always in the way. If you could just throw off those rules with a laugh and a ready sword? Oh, yeah. I get that.

And rules can be oppressive. They can smother you.

But here's the problem: God delivered a bunch of rules. And the reason you hate them is because your sinful nature can't stand the thought of God being right. It can't stand the thought that maybe, just maybe, God's rules work. That the world would be so much better if we all lived by them.

And if "we" should live by them, that means "I" should live by them, too.

But I don't wanna.

See, these rules are only oppressive if you are convinced that God is bad. If God truly is good, if God truly is *love*, then his rules are good, too. If God is good *to* you, then what God says is good *for* you.

When we find the idea of a dashing rogue that can wink at the rules so attractive, we reveal something very wrong in ourselves: We wish we could be that way with God. We like rogues because we want to be like them.

So, what do we do then? Do we just say, "Yep, God's oppressive, and I want to be a rogue"?

Romans 7:16 says, "Now if I do what I do not want to do, I agree with the law that it is good." Have you ever found yourself doing something that you didn't want to do? Something that you knew was wrong? You didn't want to do that wrong thing because of what you naturally know but don't like admitting: The Law really is good. Otherwise, you wouldn't be arguing with yourself over whether to follow it.

It's not the Law that oppresses. It's our sins. After all, "everyone who commits sin is a slave of sin." (John 8:43) Talk about oppressive!

The bad boy is convinced that what God says is bad. That's why he rejects the Law.

But you know better, don't you? You've seen how good God is. After all, "For we do not have a high priest who is unable to sympathize with our weaknesses, but one who has been tempted in every way as we are, yet without sin" (Hebrews 4:15). Jesus is so good that he never fell for any temptation. And rather than taking his goodness and going home to heaven, he gave that goodness to us.

And then he went and freed you from your sins. Instead of oppressing you, he gave you freedom by taking your chains for you.

You have his record of goodness.

You're not the "bad boy." You know better than that. You know that the Law was given by a God who loved you so much he kept the Law in your place.

And if the Law is good, why fight against it?

Prayer: Father, I do not always believe you are good. So often I think you are oppressive. Instead of oppressing me, you freed me from my sin. When I am tempted to complain or turn against you, remind me of how good you are. Remind me of your forgiveness. Hold me in the palm of your hand, Lord. Amen.

Men in Tights

OK, sure, rebelling against God isn't good. But what about dashing rogues that are good guys? What about Robin Hood? I mean, come on – he had it all. Archery. Swordplay. A wit sharper than a rapier.

Let's go back to that question: Is God good?

OK. Hopefully, we're on the same page when I say: Yes, God is good.

So that leads to the next question: Who put the government where it is? Romans 13 tells us: "Let everyone submit to the governing authorities, since there is no authority except from God." Seems straightforward, huh?

> *Government is God's good gift, even if the government is bad.*

Yeah, but what about –

Oh. Romans 13 keeps going: "and the authorities that exist are instituted by God."

OK. Sure. I get that. But what about –

"So then, the one who resists the authority is opposing God's command, and those who oppose it will bring judgment on themselves."

Oh, come *on*. Surely you can't be serious!

I am serious. And don't call me Shirley.

Look, Robin Hood was rebelling against Prince John. Now, you could argue that Prince John himself had rebelled against his brother, sure. But Prince John, no matter how badly he mistreated the peasants, was nothing like the guy who was in charge when Paul wrote those verses from Romans.

A little nobody named Nero.

Ever hear of him? Rumors say he fiddled while Rome burned. Now while that's a legend of relatively dubious origin, we do know that Nero hated Christians and used them as the scapegoat when Rome did burn. One of the things he did to punish them was dip them in tar, put them in cages, and use them as tiki torches for his dinner parties.

He wasn't exactly a good guy, you know?

And yeah. Paul says that we should obey the earthly authorities because God put them there.

But why would God put that guy in charge?

But why would God put *that guy* in charge?

He kept law and order. He made it *generally* safe for people to survive. He made it so that Christians were able to talk about Jesus to other people. He made it so that there wasn't just sheer chaos everywhere. In other words, God used a terrible man to bless the world with more opportunities to hear about Jesus.

Government is God's good gift, even if the government is bad.

And the reason it's a good gift is because God is good. God don't give bad gifts; we just don't always (or often) realize how good they are.

So yeah. Robin Hood? Great stuff for movies and books. I don't blame you if you even have a favorite Robin Hood. (Errol Flynn or the Disney version with the foxes for me.) But realize that when we rebel against the government, even if the people in charge of the government are evil, we're really rebelling against God.

Instead, look at Jesus: He was the victim of a terrible government. And more than one, too! But he submitted – so he was able to die for you, to take your sins of rebellion away. He did what we have never done: submitted to evil so that great, great good could come.

Instead, look at Jesus: He was the victim of a terrible government. And more than one, too! But he submitted...

He did that for you.

So be blown away. You don't need to rob from the rich to give to the poor. You have a Savior who submitted for you, so that you see how good our God is.

Prayer: Father, forgive me. So often I chafe under human rules and human rulers. I see their evil and don't trust that you could make good come even from this. Help me to love you and stand in awe of your love. Grow my trust in you, that even here, even with governments that I cannot see any good in, you are still in control and know what you're doing. Amen.

The Best Toys

Come on, admit it: rogues are awesome because of how good they are with their weapons. If you've ever seen it, think of *the* sword fight in *The Princess Bride*. If you've never seen it, get thee to YouTube or a library or something and watch it. The thing's amazing. Well worth geeking out over.

The entire fight, the Man in Black and Inigo are trading quips, but they're also constantly outwitting each other with their swordplay. They know all the moves, how to counter them, how to fight against each other in ways that show both have trained for years.

But in that movie, Inigo hasn't just trained. He also has his father's sword, of which the Man in Black has never seen its like. Training and a superb weapon make for a deadly enemy. And rogues, well, you don't want them fighting against you.

Do you wish you could do that? Be trained in using a weapon so you could be deadly with it?

You can!

> *The only weapon is the sword of the Spirit – which is the word of God.*

Ephesians 6 talks about the armor of God. I'm not going to go deep into it, except for this one verse, which is Ephesians 6:7: "Take the helmet of salvation and the sword of the Spirit— which is the word of God."

The only weapon is the sword of the Spirit – which is the word of God.

You have been given a weapon, and it's your Bible. OK, please, don't run around bludgeoning people on the head with your Bible. I suspect you already know that. Don't use me as an excuse to start doing it, all right?

But God's Word is a dangerous weapon. Hebrews 4:12 says, "For the word of God is living and effective and sharper than any double-edged sword, penetrating as far as the separation of soul and spirit, joints and marrow. It is able to judge the thoughts and intentions of the heart."

Think about how effective a weapon that is: it judges the thoughts and intentions of the heart. Han Solo's blaster can kill people, but it can't judge them. Inigo Montoya might be seeking revenge for his fallen father, but his blade can't cut apart soul and spirit. The Bible is an insanely powerful weapon. Overpowered, even. What do you do with a weapon like that?

If you're smart, you use it on yourself first.

You point it at yourself and see all your sin. That's what the Law in the Bible does: it reveals every time you've failed. And it will destroy you.

Or, rather, it will destroy the old you.

Because this weapon also creates new life in you. That's something no other weapon has ever done. And that new life rejoices and gives thanks to Jesus. That's what the Gospel does: it announces what Jesus has done as your substitute.

The Bible is dangerous because it kills the old you and creates a new you. And that weapon in your hands? It can be used in the exact same way on others. God's Word is a dangerous, dangerous weapon!

But... it takes training. Inigo trained for years. He studied the same forms over and over again. You: do the same with the Bible. Train. Go over the basics over and over again. See the Law at work in your life. See the Gospel bring you new life.

And you've got a pretty cool weapon, huh?

Prayer: Lord, you have given me a weapon sharper than any double-edged sword when you gave me the Bible. Thank you for using this Word on me to kill the old me and create a new faith in my heart. Help me to value this gift. Train me in it, Lord, so I may use it faithfully. Amen.

Trope Nine

Time Travel

"THIS IS *NOT* WHAT I EXPECTED."

Trope 9: Time Travel

Invaders... from the Future!

Cadmus convulsed as the rift closed behind him.

He hated time travel.

Well, at least it paid the bills. As his muscles finally stopped twitching, he hauled himself to his feet. "Begin recording," he commanded and waited for the soft ping telling him the tracker had complied. "Atmosphere is clean here. Might cause a problem for some of the settlers, but it looks like it isn't anything our smog machines can't fix. Oh, man. The view."

He paused the report, taking in the mountains around him for the first time. This was beautiful. Pristine.

Cadmus took a deep breath.

Yeah. Way cleaner than home.

And then he noticed the village below him. A few people rode on horses here. A blacksmith's hut belched smoke as the forge got up to temperature. He counted the buildings; probably a settlement of four hundred or so.

This is exactly what the Firm wanted: Nice areas to set down colony pods. Take over the nice, clean Earth of the past. And since all it would do was create an alternate earth, their future would still be secure. The perfect way to ease overcrowding and find new natural resources, all in one. And they could convince themselves they were doing their primitive ancestors a favor, giving them a hand up with better tech.

Cadmus took another deep breath.

Exactly what the Firm wanted.

Not what he wanted, though. He wanted to stop having to pay for his air. He wanted to get out of debt to the Firm. He wanted to stop time traveling.

He contemplated the tracker on his wrist.

It was bonded to his skin and his bone, wrapping around his nerves all the way to his spinal column. It could never be removed – not unless someone took off his arm. And as long as he had it, the Firm recorded his every movement.

What to do?

He could always go down to the blacksmith and have him tear off his arm.

Yeah. Like that was an option.

Cadmus hated time travel. But he hated himself more. "Initial reaction to jump: This looks perfect for settlement. I plan to remain here the requisite ten years for a full survey. A more thorough report will be forthcoming."

And now the worst part: get to know the natives. Find out how good they are.

And all the time, knowing he was going to destroy them soon, when the settlers from the future arrived.

This Trope is All about Time

Space isn't big enough for us. We need to explore time as well!

Well, maybe it's not exploration. Maybe it's more accidental.

Or maybe it's intended for some sort of job, like going back in time just an hour at a time so you can go to extra classes at school.

Or maybe you're just a madman with a box.

Any which way, you're traveling through time to visit different times. Sometimes people use a time machine. Sometimes it's a portal. Sometimes people just meditate and slip through the illusion of time to be elsewhen.

Any which way, in this trope, it's all about being at a time other than you would normally be.

Meant for Another Time

But why time travel? What problem is it trying to solve?

In many stories, it might be that we have a fascination with the past. In Wendy Nikel's novel *The Continuum*, people pay money to take vacations in other times. Maybe they want to visit the *Titanic*. Maybe they want to visit the Old West. And sometimes, well, they get so enamored with the past they just don't want to leave.

After all, other times *must* be better than this one, right?

You ever hear something like that? "Things were better in the old days." We look at the past and think, "Things were simpler. We didn't have the same problems. Sure, it wasn't perfect, but it was a lot better than this!"

> It doesn't matter when you are. We are by nature dead in our sins.

Or maybe we look to the future. "We'll have this problem solved by then!" And sure – we've been able to solve a lot of problems, haven't we? We can treat so many more diseases. Transportation is so much faster. And I personally love the magical computer box we call a phone. If today is so much better than yesterday, can you imagine how much better tomorrow will be?

It's true that different times really are different. But, as Ecclesiastes 1:9-10 says, "What has been is what will be, and what has been done is what will be done; there is nothing new under the sun. Can one say about anything, 'Look, this is new'? It has already existed in the ages before us." Some things don't change.

For instance, all people of every time are sinful. Not just "a little sinful." Ephesians 2:1-3 says, "And you were dead in your trespasses and sins in which you previously lived according to the ways of this world, according to the ruler of the power of the air, the spirit now working in the disobedient. We too all previously lived among them in our fleshly desires, carrying out the inclinations of our flesh and thoughts, and we were by nature children under wrath as the others were also."

It doesn't matter when you are. We are by nature *dead* in our sins. Humans are broken by sin. We all deserve death. It doesn't matter if you live today, 1500 BC, or AD 2476. Humans are sinful.

And what that means is that in every era, you will find people abusing one another. You will find inequality. You will find pain and sorrow and sickness and death.

Now, what *form* that abuse and inequality and pain and sorrow and sickness and death takes may change. The forms of racism we see in the United States today often look very different than they did in the 1800's. It doesn't mean there's no more racism; it just looks different. While child abuse is much more frowned upon than it used to be (and thank God for that!), there's still child abuse. While we have found ways to treat many kinds of cancer, we still have plenty of sicknesses we can't cure.

What that means is that if you like time travel because you think another era is so much better... you're wrong. Sorry. That era had just as much suffering as now. It just looks different.

> *First, let's not romanticize any time period that we're not living in.*

Is it fair to say that you think you'd prefer it somewhen else? Yeah, I think that's fair. There are certain parts of certain eras that appeal to me. I love the sheer courage of the early church, as the Gospel spread so quickly. I love the idea of living in the future when we might have flying cars! ("Where we're going, we don't need roads!")

But we need to be careful of a few different things here:

First, let's not romanticize any time period that we're not living in. Can we appreciate the differences? Most definitely. You like the wardrobes of people in other time periods? Live it up! (I personally have garb for when I visit my local Renaissance Faire, though I know the shoes I wear are far comfier than most people had back then!) But instead of placing it on a pedestal, let's appreciate what's there while also noting that they struggled with sin just as much as we do.

Second, let's appreciate when we are right now. God has placed us each when we are on purpose. God didn't say, "Oh, this human? They can go whenever. Doesn't matter." No, God knew you and placed you not just *where* you are, but also *when* you are. You have a purpose here and now. When God says, "We know that all things work together for the good of those who love God, who are called according to his purpose" (Romans 8:28), he is also talking about when and where you live. If you would rather be somewhen else, you're telling God, "Yeah, I think you messed up putting me in the twenty-first century. Probably the first mistake you made, though, so don't worry about it."

> *Second, let's appreciate when we are right now.*

God didn't make a mistake putting you here. He knew what he was doing.

If I love time travel stories because I think those other times are better, I need to check myself. If I'm unhappy here and now, it's a good bet I'll be unhappy in other times as well, because every time has its own fill of sin and sorrow.

But here's the good news: As much as every time has sin and sorrow, when Jesus died, he died for every moment in history. Even if you traveled through time, you could never get away from God's love. Romans 8:38-39 says, "For I am persuaded that neither death nor life, nor angels nor rulers, nor things present nor things to come, nor powers, nor height nor depth, nor any other created thing will be able to separate us from the love of God that is in Christ Jesus our Lord."

No created thing can separate you from the love of God that is in Christ Jesus.

God created time.

Time cannot separate you from God's love. And how did he show you that love? By knowing you in all your sins, no matter when you committed them, and loving you enough to take the punishment from you and put it on himself at the cross.

And no time travel can remove you from his reach.

What Was It like Then?

There are other reasons to time travel, though! Maybe it's not that you think another time is better than this one. Maybe it's just curiosity! What does a dinosaur's skin feel like? What did Jesus say when he spoke in all those synagogues? What will lavender grown on other planets taste like?

And God created us with this sense of wonder. That wonder is not a bad thing! (And if you're traveling as a companion to a Time Lord, all the better!)

But... this then becomes very similar to our discussion of space. I'd suggest checking out that trope and just replacing "other planets" with "other times", and you'll end up in the right place!

Don't Mess up the Time Stream!

Of course, if you're going to time travel, you better not mess with anything in the past. Ray Bradbury's story "A Sound of Thunder" is very explicit with this; if you do as little as crush a butterfly in the past, it can have disastrous consequences in the present. *Back to the Future* showed how even showing up at the wrong time could erase you from history. So many science fiction shows have taken this route. There are entire series based around the idea of maintaining the time stream. (One of my favorites is an old paperback book series called *The Man from T.E.R.R.A.*)

Unless, of course, God intended you to change the timeline that way...

If I take all those science fiction stories at face value, I think it would be quite stressful to time travel. Can you imagine having to be so careful with what words you say, what you touch, even simply where you stand, because it might change the world you left behind?

But there's an interesting supposition in almost every one of those stories: There's a way things are *supposed* to go.

A fantastic comic book story that took place in various *X-Men* comics was entitled "After Xavier: The Age of Apocalypse." In that story, a time-traveling character accidentally kills the founder of the X-Men before he had the chance to start the team. Now living in a nightmare alternate timeline, the entire storyline centered on the main characters putting things right.

> *But don't panic. God takes everything and works for the good of those who love him.*

… "putting things right."

Again, you have that assumption that there's a way things are *supposed* to go.

See, one of the neatest things about this trope is that there's this idea that there is a "supposed to." Sometimes that's phrased as "the best reality" or even just "how things used to be," but at its core is this idea that there is one way things are supposed to go.

It's really neat noticing that idea and knowing that it's a reflection of something God said that we already mentioned in this trope: "We know that all things work together for the good of those who love God, who are called according to his purpose" (Romans 8:28). And that means that any change that occurs *would* be worse, at least in the big picture!

Unless, of course, God intended you to change the timeline that way...

The TV show *Futurama* had a lot of fun with time travel in the episode "Roswell that Ends Well." In that episode, Professor Farnsworth warns Fry, "For example, if you killed your grandfather, you'd cease to exist!"

Fry responds, "But existing is basically all I do!"

Sure, bad things might happen if you tamper with the time stream. But in that same episode, Professor Farnsworth warns, "You mustn't interfere with the past! Don't do anything that affects anything, unless it turns out you were supposed to do it, in which case for the love of God, don't not do it!"

But don't panic. God takes everything and works for the good of those who love him. Even changes in time.

How do I know?

Because God invented time. He's not bound by time; he exists outside of it. He can see all of time from every angle. Even if time travel is possible, God already knows about any change that may happen and has made it so that this is the best reality.

So, if you find yourself time traveling for any reason, yeah, don't be careless. Please don't kill your grandfather. But also, don't stress out. You don't have to panic. God's still there with you in that other time, and he'll work out everything for your good.

Grandfather Paradoxes and the Modern Christian

And of course, sometimes it's not even that confusing. Sometimes we want to change the past because we know something terrible happened. Maybe we want to save JFK from assassination. Maybe we want to stop the bubonic plague. Maybe we know we made a mistake when we dated that person and just want to save ourselves a lot of heartache.

> *So, if you find yourself time traveling for any reason, yeah, don't be careless.*

We just said that we don't have to worry about changing the past because God works everything out for our good. But... what if we're *trying* to change the past?

Let's go back to that Bible verse one more time: "We know that all things work together for the good of those who love God, who are called according to his purpose" (Romans 8:28).

If that promise is true, I have no reason to change the past. Right now, I live in the timeline I am meant to live in, and it is turning out in the best possible way. That doesn't mean everything that happens to me is good, but with God in control, I know it will turn out for my good. I may not know how until heaven, and that's okay. I know I can trust the God who gave himself to death for me. If he's willing to go that far, of course he is able to order my life for my good.

Rather than trying to change the past, how about using what God has given me now to serve him and my neighbor? Yes, that most certainly includes taking care of my own body and life so that I'm enabled to serve others! But I'm not out to change God's plan for my life. Rather, I trust his plans as I serve him.

Let's dig just a little deeper, though. Why would I want to change the past? Probably because I'm convinced things would turn out better if things went differently. That I or others can escape some form of sorrow if things go differently.

But, as we talked about earlier in this chapter, we can't escape sorrow by changing where we are in time, nor by changing what happened in the past. All we can do is change the *form* of sorrow in our lives.

> There is a place and a time you will escape all sorrow, though.

There is a place and a time you will escape all sorrow, though. And that day is coming. You can't alter it: Jesus will return, and on that day all who know him will be brought to heaven, where he will wipe every tear from your eyes. Every tear. Tears from your past. Tears from your present. They will all go. You will never see them again.

You cannot create this reality through time travel or any other trope.

Only Jesus can. Only Jesus has. And he did it by dying for you, taking the death you earned, taking all your condemnation, and giving you his perfect record.

Using Time Travel to Share Jesus

If you could live at any time, when would be? Why is that?

I want to take a guess at something: There's something here you don't like, and you think it's fixed, or at least better in that other time. Am I right?

I guess I'm kind of like that. I wish I could get away from the brokenness I have here. But there's only one time like that, where everything is perfect... and that's at the end of time. But I know I'm going to see it. I'll be there at the end of time, no time travel required.

That's because Jesus promised I'd be there. Let me tell you about it...

Are You Pondering What I'm Pondering?

The next time you encounter a story with time travel, ask:

- ✓ If the characters chose to time travel, why did they do so? Are they looking for a better place, or are they simply curious?

- ✓ Are the characters concerned about changing time? Why?

- ✓ Are the characters trying to change time? What do they expect the outcome to be, and why do they think it will end that way?

- ✓ Is there a way things are "supposed to be" if time is changed? How do the characters know it is "supposed" to be that way?

The next time you enjoy a story with time travel, ask:

- ✓ What am I enjoying most about this story?

- ✓ Do I want to change time? If so, why?

- ✓ Am I content with when God has put me? If not, why not?

- ✓ How can I know that this is the time God intended me to be? How can I grow in contentment?

Meditations on Time Travel

If You Could Choose When You Were Born...

A lot of us wish we could visit other times. Maybe you even wish you were born in some other time. Imagine what it would be like to be born at a time of exploration before the planet was mapped. Imagine being born during the height of the Roman Empire, or in Edo period Japan. How about flying to the future when British people live on space whales? When would you choose to be born, if you could choose?

> *Jesus looked over all of history and selected exactly when he would be born.*

One person did choose. Jesus looked over all of history and selected exactly when he would be born.

I have to admit, I'm not sure I would have chosen when he did. His chosen people weren't in great shape; after all, they were a nation controlled by the Roman Empire. Not a lot of people seemed to be paying attention to God's promises, or at least not in the way God intended them. There was no social media, and news traveled so much slower than it does now. I would have picked a time with a lot more choices for entertainment, faster communication, and probably air conditioning.

Hey, I like my air conditioning.

But Jesus chose very differently than I would have. Galatians 4:4-5 says, "When the time came to completion, God sent his Son, born of a woman, born under the law, to redeem those under the law, so that we might receive adoption as sons."

God had made promises for millennia that he was coming. He waited and watched, orchestrating world events and personal events so that his promise could be kept. And when everything came together, God kept his promise. Jesus was born. He lived. He died. He lived again.

He lived at a time when there was a common language over a good chunk of the world. He arrived at a time when there were good roads and relatively safe traveling conditions. He came to a world that was hungry for a Savior, even if they didn't understand what that Savior would be like. In other words, he chose to be born at just the right moment.

And did you notice why he was born when he was born?

When I think about when I would want to be born, it's all about my comfort. (Remember the thing with the air conditioning?)

But Jesus – he was born to redeem us. To buy us back from our sin.

That's why he chose the place and time he chose: It was the best time to save us.

So even though I would have picked differently, I'm grateful that Jesus chose the time he did. It was just right.

Prayer: Jesus, other times fascinate me. I wish I could time travel. Sometimes I wish I was born at a different time. But you chose when you were born, and you chose a time that was perfect to save me. Thank you. Thank you for thinking of my rescue when you chose when to live. Amen.

Everywhen

When I describe God, I might use words like omniscient, omnipotent, and omnipresent. Those words mean that God is all-knowing, all-powerful, and he is everywhere. Sometimes we include another word to describe God: He's eternal. Isaiah 9:6 describes God this way: "For a child will be born for us, a son will be given to us, and the government will be on his shoulders. He will be named Wonderful Counselor, Mighty God, Eternal Father, Prince of Peace." That means he's not just everywhere; he's everywhen.

Right now, God is at the dawn of time, setting the stars in place. Right now, he's with David as he slays Goliath. Right now, he's at Jesus's baptism. Right now, he's with you as you read this book. Right now, God is at all those times.

Because God is everywhen, when he makes a promise, you can trust him. He's already kept it.

Confused?

Yeah. It's a hard concept to wrap a brain around.

The best illustration I've ever seen of what "eternal" is like comes from *Star Trek: Deep Space Nine*. Yes, I'm a geek, but you knew that already.

In that show, there's a race of "non-linear" aliens. They don't experience time as first this, then that, then that. Everything happens at once for them. There is no past or future; everything is right now. And when the main characters of the show encounter them, they appear to move around in their own timelines. It's a fascinating concept, and I'm almost certain the writers of the show weren't thinking about the Christian God when they wrote it, but hey, it still makes a good illustration.

So right now, God is standing with you as you die. He is already carrying you to heaven. And because he already knows the end of your story, because he's already there, when he says to you, "I will take care of everything you need," to him, he's already kept that promise. In fact, he's keeping it right now. When he says, "I forgive you all your sins," right now, to him, he's paying for your sins. It's already done. When he says, "Trust me," he's already proven it to you a million times, and he's proving it right now over and over again.

Because God is everywhen, when he makes a promise, you can trust him. He's already kept it.

There is a scary part of this aspect of God, though. Because he's everywhen, it means that right now he's standing with you when you did... that. You know. That thing that you're ashamed of. That thing that is wrong, and you know it is wrong, but you did it anyway.

God is standing there, right now, watching you do it.

But at that same moment, Jesus is dying for you. At that moment. And Jesus is thinking of you when he goes to the cross, saying, "Yes, for this sin, too."

So you can take comfort that God is eternal. He's everywhen.

Prayer: God, you are everywhen, and it's hard for me to understand that fully. But even as I struggle to understand it, I take comfort in the fact that though you are right now seeing me as I sin over and over again, right now you are paying for my sins and forgiving me. Help me to rejoice in your power. Amen.

Tell the Future!

There's plenty of time travel stories where someone from the future uses knowledge of what's going to happen to their benefit. Maybe it's knowing the sports scores to become rich. Maybe it's using that knowledge to prevent a disaster. And sometimes those people from the future tell the future and become prophets. (SPOILER ALERT! Skip the rest of the paragraph if you want to prevent spoiler knowledge!) Jeffrey Sinclair in *Babylon 5* does this. He goes back in time to help the Minbari race get ready to fight the Shadows in the future, and in the process he becomes their primary religious leader.

The Bible has some very specific prophecies. Read Psalm 22. There are so many specific references to Jesus dying on the cross, it's hard to imagine it wasn't written by someone who saw it with their own eyes. Isaiah 53 is another chapter like that. It describes Jesus so well!

Did David, who wrote Psalm 22, or Isaiah, who wrote Isaiah 53 – did they see Jesus die on the cross? Were they time travelers?

> When Jesus speaks about not losing you, because he knows your own name, well, he's already done it.

Well, no. But the person who told them about what would happen saw Jesus die on the cross. 2 Peter 1:20-21 says, "Above all, you know this: No prophecy of Scripture comes from the prophet's own interpretation, because no prophecy ever came by the will of man; instead, men spoke from God as they were carried along by the Holy Spirit."

The Holy Spirit told them what would happen. And the Holy Spirit, as he told Isaiah and David what to write, was watching Jesus die. The Holy Spirit, as a person of the Trinity, is eternal. (Check out the last devotion if you skipped it or need a refresher.) These prophecies are so accurate not because David and Isaiah were time travelers. They're accurate because God is accurate, and he told them what to write.

What does this mean for you? It means that those prophecies that haven't happened yet are just as reliable as Psalm 22 or Isaiah 53. When Jesus speaks about returning on the last day and judging the world, he's speaking from experience. Because he's eternal, he's already done it. When Jesus speaks about not losing you, because he knows your own name, well, he's already done it. He's speaking from experience!

In other words, God's eternal – and because of that, we can trust his promises – both the promises he already fulfilled in Jesus's life, death, and resurrection, and the promises he makes for our own lives.

No time travel needed.

Prayer: Lord, thank you for giving us prophecies about your Son so that we can know more about him and trust you more. Grow my trust in you, so that I hold firm in your promises. Amen.

Trope Ten

Alternate Universes

"DON'T TRY THE GREATEST OF ALL TIME UNIVERSE.
I WAS A GOAT FOR A MONTH."

Trope 10: Alternate Universes

Let's Jump the Timeline

Ten years. Ten years he'd lived here, and now it was time to send the final report.

Cadmus hadn't yet, though. He looked one last time down the valley.

Nora was there. And their children.

No way he was going to send a report that said that everything was perfect for settlement from the future. He wasn't going to create yet one more universe with settlers from his timeline. One more world for them to destroy.

Nope. He was going to destroy it first.

The tracker on the back of his hand beeped at him.

"Report not able to be sent yet. Please hold one hour until I'm in a better position."

The tracker blinked red twice, and then blue.

Yep. He'd held off long enough. They were getting impatient in the future. They needed to know if they could send their colony pod. Was it good enough? Everything said it should be good enough. His previous reports – before he'd ever met Nora – said it was good enough.

Cadmus turned from the valley and ran back to his transmit site. Back to where he'd left his stash of tech, phased just out of sight unless you had the key.

The key that sat on the back of his hand in the transmitter.

He climbed. He climbed as fast as he could. His calloused hands were soon scratched. Soon bleeding. He kept moving. Ten years here had left him in such good health. His muscles had hardened. He'd gotten used to the sun.

But he was ten years older, too.

He wheezed by the time he made it to the site. He should have done this yesterday.

He couldn't leave Nora's smile.

But now... now it might be too late. He'd waited too long.

He waved his tracker and muttered the code words. The tech phased back into current reality. Where was it now? He rushed past the rations and the various atmospheric processors.

There. The teleporter. Just in case he needed to check out more of the planet. Well, not just in case. He was supposed to do that anyway.

But now it was his key to stopping the invasion. He ripped open its cover and worked his magic. He knew how to repair all these things.

He also knew how to sabotage them.

His tracker flashed red again. A little stab of pain, right to his spinal column.

Time to report. They weren't going to wait any longer.

He set the teleporter for the coordinates he wanted to go to. The site that New York would be built on in just a hundred years. There were people there now, of course, but not a lot.

Thank God.

The teleporter blinked its displeasure.

The tracker stabbed its displeasure at him.

"Goodbye, Nora," he whispered. If he didn't teleport himself, the equipment wouldn't work. He didn't have the time to try and go around that protection in the system. And he so teleported himself, along with all the equipment. Every last gram of matter from the future.

And when it all reached the site of New York, everything teleported into the same space. No phasing. Just on top of one another.

The resultant explosion left a crater where no city could ever be built.

And Cadmus's future never came to be. He shunted this entire timeline over. And with that future never happening now, there would be no invaders from that future. With his last breath, he'd created an alternate timeline.

And his wife Nora would never, ever know what had happened to her odd but loving husband. Some nights she would wonder, though, what would have happened if he had never left her…

What if?

A Multiversal Trope

What if…?

This trope asks a dangerous question. What if you turned left instead of right? What if that person had been born a boy instead of a girl? What if that person had been voted in as president instead? What if we all had goatees? How would the world be different?

This trope asks a dangerous question. What if you turned left instead of right?

Alternate history is a thriving subgenre. Harry Turtledove has written quite a few of these books, with questions asked ranging from "What if the South won the Civil War?" to "What if aliens invaded during World War II?" Eric Flint wrote a series of novels based around the question, "What would happen if a modern town from the southern states was transported to 1632?" People love doing this with real history.

Of course, there are lots of long-running science fiction franchises that also thrive on this concept. *Star Trek* has more than a few episodes that revolve around alternate universes. *Stargate SG-1* used the alternate universe concept to ratchet up the tension in one of its major storylines. The TV show *Sliders* was entirely based around that concept, as the main characters jumped from universe to universe every episode. And *Into the Spider-Verse* obviously plays in this trope quite a bit!

Even non-science fiction shows have used the alternate universe concept. *Friends* had one episode answer a bunch of "what if" questions. You could argue that *It's a Wonderful Life* is an alternate universe story, showing what would have happened had George Bailey never lived. You could even argue that *A Christmas Carol* pioneered the use of alternate futures.

Comic books love addressing "what if" scenarios. Marvel Comics even had a long-running series entitled *What If?* X-Men comics frequently use the alternate universe trope, perhaps most successfully in *Days of the Future Past* (even making it into the movies) and *After Xavier: Age of Apocalypse*.

> *Comic books love addressing "what if" scenarios.*

Fantasy stories don't typically use alternate universes as much, though it does happen. Roger Zelazny's *Amber* series features alternate universes in a major way. *Shrek Forever After* also asks the question, "What if Shrek never lived?"

(If you can't tell by this list that's rather lengthier than many in this book, this is a favorite trope of mine. Any time *Star Trek* had an alternate universe episode, it never failed to be among my favorites.)

Really, depending how far you bend the alternate universe trope, you could define any fiction as fitting here. "What if the Grinch stole Christmas?" But for our discussion here, we'll be focusing on stories that ask a "what if" that deviates either from actual history or the established history of a given setting.

But all in all, the alternate universe trope presenting a different universe that shows "what if" is a popular trope across the board.

The Most Dangerous Question

"What if" may be the most dangerous question in the world. It takes you down so many pathways and introduces you to so many worlds.

It leads you to ask; what's important to history? Is one person really that important, or would removing them change nothing? Is history so precarious that stepping on a butterfly changes everything, or is it so settled that if you stopped a key event from occurring, something else would happen to stabilize the timeline? Are there fixed points in time?

Do you ever ask questions like that? Do you wish you could see this other universe right around the corner?

If something changed... would life be better?

So, obviously, I'm a geek. And I've considered my own life: if certain things were different, would my life be better? What if I hadn't made that mistake? What if I had resisted that temptation? What if I chose to go into television production instead of being a pastor?

Do you ever ask questions like that? Do you wish you could see this other universe right around the corner?

And our fascination with alternate universes reveals something: We long for things to be different. We want things to be *better* than they are now. It doesn't matter what your background is or what you believe about the world: we have this urge, this innate sense, that things are not what they should be.

Of course, that sense is right. The world is not what it should be. Ever since Adam and Eve chose to rebel against their creator, this world has been broken. We can taste little sips of goodness here and there. We get the feeling that things were better once, and maybe they could be again, but they are not the way they should be now.

And so, to a point, alternate universes serve as a way to find that better place.

It's interesting, though, that in most media, alternate universes are *worse* than our current reality. In the *Star Trek: The Next Generation* episode "Yesterday's Enterprise," we are introduced to an alternate universe where the Federation is being destroyed by the Klingon Empire. In "Days of the Future Past" (the comic version, not the movie version), the X-Men are hunted down and destroyed. The entire point of *It's a Wonderful Life* is that the world is worse without George Bailey. It was a running joke that pretty much any scenario portrayed in the Marvel Comics series *What If?* ended in destruction.

Why do you think that in a trope that's set to explore the multiverse, so often the possibilities are bad?

Why do you think that in a trope that's set to explore the multiverse, so often the possibilities are bad?

Usually it's to heighten tension: Look how bad things could get if we fail in the normal timeline! I really doubt most storytellers are really thinking about the alternate universe on a spiritual level – they're thinking about plot and character development. They also don't want an alternate universe to overshadow their main world; if the alternate universe was better, they'd just write about that one instead!

I think that maybe there's a reflection of something real going on here, though: maybe the world we have really is the best world possible.

The Best World Possible

That's a terrifying thought, isn't it? Think about how broken this place is. Think about the abuse that happens. The horrors. The despair. How could this world possibly be the best one?

1 Timothy 2:4 says, "[God] wants everyone to be saved and to come to the knowledge of the truth."

This is the universe where the most people know Jesus.

This is the universe where God said, "I will rescue my people."

This is the universe where Jesus sacrificed himself for *you*.

If there are other universes, does that mean Jesus had to die multiple times? Or does it mean that Jesus only died in this universe for his people?

Romans 6:9-10 says, "We know that Christ, having been raised from the dead, will not die again. Death no longer rules over him. For the death he died, he died to sin once for all time; but the life he lives, he lives to God." That "once for all time" word in the Greek stresses, "once and never ever again." 1 Peter 3:18 says, "For Christ also suffered for sins once for all, the righteous for the unrighteous, that he might bring you to God."

That stresses: Jesus died once. Once for all. That's it. He only had to die once. Jesus's blood is so precious that he didn't have to die many times over and over again. That one sacrifice was enough to cover every sin ever committed by every person ever.

There is a better world. It's not an alternate universe, though.

It's a place called heaven.

So, when you encounter a story with a parallel universe, it's a neat reflection that we recognize we want to find someplace better. And should that parallel universe turn out to not be so awesome after all, it reflects the truth that this is the best possible of all worlds.

But, again, that's still depressing. This world still is broken.

And it will remain that way until Jesus returns. Though Jesus has conquered sin and death, they still run around this world until he comes back to set everything right.

In other words: There is a better world. It's not an alternate universe, though.

It's a place called heaven.

We don't need some sort of device to zap us to that place. We don't need a portal. We don't need time travel to reach branching worlds.

We have what we need to reach that better world: We have Jesus.

And that's all we need to reach that perfect place. His sacrifice was enough to buy us the ticket from this broken place to a world where God himself will wipe every tear from our eyes.

Using Alternate Universes to Share Jesus

Do you ever wish things were different here? Like, do you ever wonder, "What if...?"

I do.

I wish we lived in a better world. I just... it bugs me. So much bugs me. You?

Yeah.

But... what if there was a better world? What if there was a place that wasn't broken like this? What would you do to go there?

Well, I am going to a better world. But I didn't have to pay anything to go there.

Jesus paid for me. And he paid for you, too.

And that's all we need to reach that perfect place. His sacrifice was enough to buy us the ticket from this broken place to a world where God himself will wipe every tear from our eyes.

Are You Pondering What I'm Pondering?

The next time you encounter a story that uses an alternate universe, ask:

- ✓ What "What if" scenario is being explored here?
- ✓ Does this story make the "normal" timeline seem better in comparison? Why?
- ✓ Why did the storyteller choose to explore an alternate timeline?
- ✓ What new revelations about the normal timeline does this alternate universe bring to the table?

The next time you enjoy a story that uses an alternate universe, ask:

- ✓ What about this story draws me to it?
- ✓ Am I convinced that my life would be better in a "what if" scenario? If so, why?
- ✓ Is my enjoyment of an alternate universe an indication that I am hungering for a better place? What better place can I look forward to?
- ✓ How can I grow in my appreciation that this world is the best world, and that God himself directs its affairs?

Meditations on Alternate Universes

The Best Possible Universe

Sometimes I really, really wish I could look into alternate universes and find a different one. What universe would you live in?

The one where it snows ice cream?

The one where you got that amazing date, and it actually went well?

The one where you never got into that habit?

The one where you never did that thing you still feel guilty about?

> **But here's the amazing thing: God worked all that out for my good.**

I know there's certain things I would change if I could. I wish I lived in the universe where my middle school years were better. Though I dealt with a lot of bullies, I also gave them a lot of ammunition. I wish I had known better. I wish I hadn't messed up so badly in high school. I wish...

I wish a lot of things.

But here's the amazing thing: God worked all that out for my good. He promised as much. Romans 8:28 says, "We know that all things work together for the good of those who love God, who are called according to his purpose."

Which means that the parts of my history I wish I could change? Those parts are for my good. It's not that they are good in themselves, but God used them. He used them to bless me. To grow me. To change me into someone who follows him more closely, who stays away from sin more, who has learned wisdom.

In other words, despite my past, I am living in the best possible universe right now.

That's crazy, isn't it? That even with my messed up life... even with your messed up life... you have become the best possible version of you, because God has guided the entire process. There is no alternate universe that's better. If I could move to an alternate timeline, even if it "fixed" something that I hate, something worse would come from it. Maybe I wouldn't recognize it as worse; maybe I'd have more friends or have an easier life.

But maybe as a result I wouldn't know Jesus. Maybe because of my actions, I never told someone about Jesus, while here I did tell them.

In other words, that other universe would be worse, no matter how much better it looked.

And maybe you long for a different world because you feel guilty. You look at your past and wish you had never committed that sin. You wish you'd never hurt that person that way. When that happens, remember:

That promise where God works for your good? That's for anyone who loves him. Not just you. He'll work for good in that other person's life, too.

And this universe is so good because it is here that Jesus died for *your* sins, too. Even the ones you feel guilty about. When your heart condemns you, Jesus is bigger than your heart. There is no condemnation for you anymore.

When you long for something different, remember that this is the best universe – not because you're that awesome, but because God is that awesome about taking all the junk of this world and producing the most marvelous art. (Thanks to Rich Mullins for that phrasing!)

Prayer: Dear Father of all, sometimes I wish I could change my past. Thank you for not giving me that ability. Thank you for taking all the junk of my life and making it art. Help me to trust that you know what you're doing, even when I fail. When I feel guilty about my past and want to change it, teach me to trust you and your forgiveness. Comfort me with your grace. Amen.

Jesus Yearns

In the last devotion, we talked about how we are in the best possible universe. Sometimes it's hard to believe that. We really yearn for something else, don't we?

Did you know Jesus yearned for a different world, too? Listen to what he says in Luke 13:34: "Jerusalem, Jerusalem, who kills the prophets and stones those who are sent to her. How often I wanted to gather your children together, as a hen gathers her chicks under her wings, but you were not willing!"

Did you hear the anguish in his voice? Jesus longed for a world where people ran to him so he could protect them. He wanted a world where people knew their sin and fled to him for forgiveness. He wanted a different world.

If anyone can change time, if anyone could make this an alternate timeline, it's Jesus.

And he did.

God himself stepped into time to change everything. He didn't have to. He could have simply stayed outside time, outside this world, and watched what happened. But Jesus chose to change things.

Did you know Jesus yearned for a different world, too?

At just the right moment, he stepped into time. And his presence caused a shift in the universe: God became our brother. And he chose to die. He chose to change everything by taking not just my guilt, and not just your guilt, but the guilt of every single human who has ever lived or will ever live, and he put it on himself.

Before, there was only one way to heaven: Be perfect.

I never walked that route. I can't.

Jesus did. But when he got to heaven walking the "be perfect" route, he turned around and said, "No!" He opened up a new way. He gave us his record. So even though we didn't walk the "be perfect" road, it looks like we did. And how do we get his record?

By trusting that when Jesus died for the world, he died for *me*.

Now there's two routes to heaven: be perfect, or trust Jesus.

It's a different world, now. You live in a better world. And yes, Jesus longs for one even better, and by his actions, you have a route there – the route Jesus opened up.

Now you're on the road to a world so much better than this one. A world called heaven.

Prayer: Lord, thank you for changing the world. Thank you for longing to rescue me. Thank you for making me your own. Help me to trust you more and more, until I see you face to face in the best world of heaven. Amen.

If anyone can change time, if anyone could make this an alternate timeline, it's Jesus.

And he did.

God is Wrong.

I've said it several times now: this is the best possible universe.

You're not so sure. If this is the best universe, God made a mistake. Clearly. My life is falling apart. I'm in pain. I hurt every time I look in the mirror.

If this is the best possible universe, I want out.

I don't blame you. This world is still broken and will remain broken until Jesus returns. It does hurt in this world. A lot. I don't know your pain. I know mine. I know I've wanted to escape it so many times before. This can't possibly be the best universe. God made a mistake.

Even when you reject God, he loves you enough to do what is best for you every time.

The people of Israel sure thought so. They loved their land. They loved the temple they'd built to honor God. And then they were conquered by an invading army from Babylon. The temple was leveled. The capital city was destroyed. They were carried off to a foreign land.

Clearly God made a mistake. Clearly God was wrong. This couldn't be right.

(Never mind that the people were using the temple as a good luck charm and had rejected the true God long ago. Never mind that God had been sending warnings to them for centuries.)

But in the midst of all this pain, what does God say? Jeremiah 29:11 says, "'For I know the plans I have for you"—this is the Lord's declaration—"plans for your well-being, not for disaster, to give you a future and a hope.'"

God knew the plans he had for them. In all that pain, they turned back to him. They realized their false gods would not rescue them. And that is what true prospering is: knowing and trusting the God of grace.

And even here, in a place they didn't want to be, God hadn't abandoned them. He was with them, working through everything for their good. Even though they had rejected him, God still loved them and did everything possible to reach out to them. Even when their entire world fell apart, God was there to love them.

That's what makes this the best possible universe. Not your circumstances. Not your emotional state. These things change – trust me, I know from experience!

What makes this the best possible universe is that even when you sin, even when you reject God, he loves you enough to do what is best for you every time. He has plans for you, too – plans to prosper you. Plans for hope. Plans for a future.

Prayer: God, when I think you've messed up, when I'm convinced that you are wrong, be patient with me. I hurt. Help me in this pain. Guide me to see that even in this pain, you are good and true and love me. Amen.

Trope Eleven

The MacGuffin

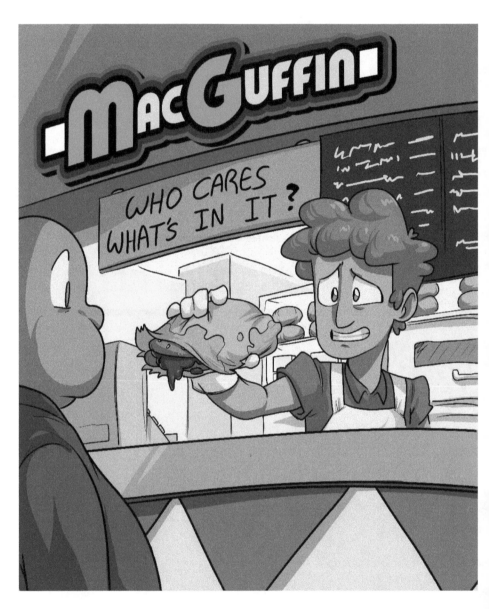

THE NEW MACGUFFIN SANDWICH.

Trope 11: The MacGuffin

Valuable Information

Listen, man, this is insane. Just insane. All right. Let me catch my breath. All right. So, I was just trying to get out of the wind, all right? That's all. Nothing important. I ducked into an alley. I thought maybe, hey, maybe I could catch my breath for a few. I don't know. Just some alley.

And then some body fell from the roof.

I screamed. I screamed, but I don't know if anyone heard me. Nobody came running to see what the matter was.

No, I mean, no, I don't know who he was. Some guy in a suit. He'd been beaten up pretty bad before he fell from how he looked. But he was still alive! He called out, barely a whisper. No one could have heard him over the wind. I couldn't. But he reached out a bloody hand, all shaking. He had a memory card. I finally caught a few words of what he was saying. Just a couple words.

I looked up to see where he fell from. There were these… these *things* looking over the edge of the building. No, they weren't people! They were, I don't know, not quite people. Like, they were pretending to be people, but they weren't good at it. Their fingers were too long, and their mouths were sideways. There were three of them, and one of them points at me, and he says something, but the wind was howling past the mouth of the alley, and I couldn't hear what he said, and I was okay with that.

The guy that fell off the roof? He coughed. He was still holding out that memory card toward me. And I panicked, right? I had no idea what was going on. So I bolted back out into the wind. I ran all the way back to my place.

And then I came here. I mean, all week I've tried to… to… But anyway, you're good with this kind of thing. You have to help me. What… what do I do now? Would the police…?

No, I didn't take the memory card! Why would I? Some guy falls off the roof – would you take whatever he gave you?

Oh, and it gets worse. Those not-quite-people? They're following me. I think. I'm not sure. I just get this feeling. And every once in a while, I'll see someone that's not right. Like they put their fingernails on upside down, or their shoulders are backwards.

And I think I know why. It's not just because I saw them. There's creepy stories all over the world about things pretending to be human.

No, they think I have the memory card. I don't have it. I don't know what's on it. But they think I have it, so they're coming after me.

Hey. Hey! Focus here. I came to you for help.

No, I'm not lying! Why would I take some bloody memory card!

You alright?

Alright, alright, I see you're busy. Maybe not feeling well. I'll go get help from someone else. Oh, no, no need. I know how to get out of your place.

Just stay there. Don't move. Hey, pal, we've been buddies a long time, but I see the green under your skin there. Something's infecting you. Just stay there. You'll be fine if I go. It's just one of the other things chasing me down now.

Just because I saw the memory card. Just because of what that guy whispered. It's not like I asked him to tell me the password for whatever's on the thing.

All because I had to go and duck into an alley.

A Sought-After Trope

Sometimes people are looking for things, and it doesn't matter what the thing is. Maybe it's secret plans. Maybe it's a lost treasure. Maybe it's a will. And sometimes it's a MacGuffin.

A MacGuffin is an item that gets the plot rolling but isn't actually important to the plot. If you could replace that same item with an egg or a lamp, and it

> *Sometimes people are looking for things, and it doesn't matter what the thing is.*

doesn't affect the story being told, you've got a MacGuffin.

If everyone's after a magic sword that's the key to defeating the bad guy, and in the end the bad guy is defeated with that sword, that's not a MacGuffin. That sword was important to the plot! You can't replace it with an egg!

But if everyone's after, say, a memory card, and what's actually on the memory card is never used in the story, well, that would be a MacGuffin!

Can We Get Some Tension Here, Please?

By simply existing, the MacGuffin can raise the tension in a story. That's useful!

Sometimes you need something to go chase, and the MacGuffin provides that. The story really isn't about the item, but about the chase itself. Maybe it's a mystery. Where did the people put the thing? Maybe it's an adventure, and the heroes have to get past all sorts of obstacles and other people looking for the item. By simply existing, the MacGuffin can raise the tension in a story. That's useful!

And that tension is what the MacGuffin is all about. It's simply an object to get things moving, even when it's not important.

One of my favorite MacGuffins isn't an object, though. In the movie *Willow*, a prophecy says that a child will cause the downfall of the evil Queen Bavmorda. The child is discovered and hidden. The entire movie revolves around protecting that baby. In the end, the queen is defeated, but the baby has nothing to do with it!

The Sorcerer's (or Philosopher's) Stone serves as a MacGuffin for the first *Harry Potter* book. Even though the villain Voldemort desperately wants the magical artifact, the device itself is never used. It's simply the object that the bad guy wants to get.

It's not always bad guys chasing the MacGuffin, though. Scrooge McDuck is often chasing after some treasure in *Duck Tales*. Sinbad wants to restore the Book of Peace in *Sinbad: Legend of the Seven*

Seas. Phineas searches for his sister's special doll in the aptly titled *Phineas and Ferb* episode, "Finding Mary McGuffin." (Incidentally, doing research, I found various ways to spell "MacGuffin.")

Why is there all this chasing around, though?

We All Chase Something

We all chase something. We believe we need *something* to make our lives work. What is it for you?

> But the thing you're chasing... will it actually fix anything for you?

Some people chase after money. Scrooge McDuck is famous for that, but it happens to nonfictional people, too. Sometimes we chase after what we think money will provide, like security or status. Maybe we want power. We want the ability to protect ourselves. Maybe we want approval. If that one person would let us be their friend, if we heard, "I'm proud of you," from that one person, everything would be all right. Or maybe you want a relationship with that one person, or maybe anyone. If you just had that romantic connection, you could be at peace.

In stories, everyone chases the MacGuffin because they think it'll provide what they need. The secret plans will give them security. The treasure will fill in a hole in their collection. The doll will show her how much I love her.

But the thing you're chasing... will it actually fix anything for you?

Let's be honest: It might well fix something short-term. That relationship might make you feel safe. The money might mean you don't have to worry about certain tensions. That approval will help you feel accepted.

But soon enough, the MacGuffin you chase isn't enough. Like Scrooge McDuck, you need to go on another journey to find the next thing that will fix everything.

One person finally gives approval... but now that person over there isn't happy with you! Now what? You got the money, but it runs out.

You got the relationship, but you find out that this person is just as sinful and broken as you are.

Now what?

Is it worth chasing a MacGuffin?

My MacGuffin!

Is it worth chasing something that will solve your problems?

Imagine that somewhere there is an object that really can fix everything. *Everything.* Maybe it's a holy grail. Would the peasants rejoice? Would it be worth the search? How far would you go to get it?

Humanity is proficient at abusing God's gifts.

Now, imagine you have the device. You've found the grail! Not just a grail-shaped beacon, but the grail itself! (And if you have no idea what I'm talking about, get thee to a screen and watch *Monty Python and the Holy Grail*. It's another movie about a MacGuffin!)

You've found a device that can wipe away all the problems of the world.

Now, be honest.

Do you think that if we had a device like that we'd abuse it?

Well, humanity is proficient at abusing God's gifts. We abuse our bodies. We abuse our planet. We abuse each other. Yeah, I'm pretty confident that we would abuse such a gift. And if it was out there, imagine how much people would scramble over each other to get it. How much would we fight to lay our hands on something that would make everything all right? Think of the fights that seem to happen every season on Black Friday.

In any story with a MacGuffin, people are fighting over it. If that's true for Scrooge McDuck or Monty Python, how much more would it happen if the object saved the world?

And in the battle for the MacGuffin, you see two fascinating reflections of the truth:

First, humans fight over anything they value. If I think something will benefit me, I will try to get it. And if you get in my way or try to get it first? It's a race or a battle.

Second, we realize that *something* out there will help us, but we don't know what it is. Often, the MacGuffin is unknown. In *Willow*, no one knows how the baby will stop the evil queen. The world doesn't know what will actually help them.

We do, though.

God Didn't Give a MacGuffin

Thank God he didn't give us a MacGuffin. He gave us himself. He didn't give us a temporary or powerless prop, something we could trade for an egg or a lamp or any old thing.

Instead of giving us some object we could lose or would have to fight over, he provides himself as the sacrifice. We don't need to discover ancient lore to uncover his whereabouts; he's present in his Word. We don't have to battle ancient traps or solve riddles to get him; Jesus gives himself freely.

And he is so, so much better than any MacGuffin.

Humanity is proficient at abusing God's gifts.

Those other things that you chase? Remember how we said that they don't last? Jesus is the same yesterday and today and forever (Hebrews 13:8). The same Jesus that died for you is the same Jesus that stands with you today. And he's not going away.

You can lose the relationship. You might drop that ancient artifact. Maybe the grail really is just a grail-shaped beacon.

But Jesus isn't someone you can lose. He walks with you through the valley of the shadow of death to bright, bright meadows on the other side (Psalm 23:4).

Using MacGuffins to Share Jesus

Don't you wish you had a device that could fix everything? How far would you go to get something like that? Would you fight off bad guys and go journeying and solve riddles?

What if it was free?

See, I have something that can conquer death. Well, not something. Someone. And that someone is named Jesus.

Are You Pondering What I'm Pondering?

The next time you experience a story with a MacGuffin, ask:

- ✓ What do people hope to gain by finding the MacGuffin?
- ✓ Does the MacGuffin actually help anyone in this story?
- ✓ What is the cost of gaining the MacGuffin?

The next time you enjoy a story that uses a MacGuffin, ask:

- ✓ What is the thing I'm seeking most in my life? How will that thing actually help me?
- ✓ What will I pay to gain that thing?
- ✓ How is Jesus better than that thing?

Meditations on MacGuffins

Your Cross Won't Save You

Have you seen them? "The Search for... the Lost Ark of the Covenant!" Or maybe "The Search for... Noah's Ark!" Or was it "The Search for... the Shroud of Turin!"?

Christians have looked for MacGuffins before. Europe is littered with relics supposedly brought from Israel. And these items, in theory, can work miracles.

Maybe you notice by my phrasing with "supposedly" and "in theory," I really don't believe that these relics have a lot of power. Even so, Christian churches have battled over such relics. (Though it's not science fiction or fantasy, Ellis Peters's *A Morbid Taste for Bones* presents a murder mystery around people battling to take possession of a relic in the medieval church.)

That cross necklace? It can serve a purpose. It can remind you that Jesus purchased you.

Even if you don't have a relic like St. Not-Appearing-In-This-Book's Massive Sourcebook of Soup, you might have something you treat like a relic. Maybe you've got something you depend on to rescue you. Do you have a cross necklace you need to wear? Or maybe the fact that you have a Bible next to your bed makes you feel better. Is it that you have membership at a church?

None of those things will save you. You may have fought for them. They very well may have sentimental value. But they won't save you.

So, what will save you?

You've made it this far into the book. You already know the answer.

Jesus has saved you. It is his death and resurrection that have taken away your sin. That's how he prepared a place in heaven for you: by dying as your substitute.

That cross necklace? It can serve a purpose. It can remind you that Jesus purchased you. That has value! The necklace by itself isn't a magic talisman, though! The necklace won't protect you.

The Bible next to your bed? It doesn't help you unless you read it! It's not a book of magic spells to get you what you want. It's God's history of human sin and his forgiveness.

Church membership? That's awesome. It shows your commitment to gathering around the Bible with other Christians and binds you together. The membership won't get you to heaven or forgive any sins, though!

These items are blessings, but don't let them become MacGuffins. Instead, keep Jesus as your treasure.

1 Peter 1:18-19 says, "For you know that you were redeemed from your empty way of life inherited from your ancestors, not with perishable things like silver or gold, but with the precious blood of Christ, like that of an unblemished and spotless lamb."

Jesus is more precious, more powerful, and more lasting than any MacGuffin you could chase. Which means he's more than a MacGuffin. He's your Savior.

Prayer: Lord, I've found myself depending on the blessings you give to rescue me instead of depending on you. Help me to use blessings as they're meant to be used, but to depend on you. You have rescued me, and for that, I thank and praise you! Amen.

Jesus is more precious, more powerful, and more lasting than any MacGuffin you could chase.

The Jesus MacGuffin

Is Jesus your MacGuffin?

Okay, so, a MacGuffin is something a bunch of people chase after that, in the end, really could be anything. It doesn't matter what the object is. If everyone in *Monty Python and the Holy Grail* had been searching for radioactive potatoes, it wouldn't have changed the movie a whole lot. They'd do all the same things to find what they were looking for.

And yes. Jesus can be your MacGuffin.

Basically, for some people, if you replace their picture of Jesus with a picture of a talking French fry, it wouldn't change anything. They'd do the same things and believe the same things, because for them Jesus is just a MacGuffin.

Is Jesus your MacGuffin? Is he replaceable to you?

Maybe they replace Jesus with "going to church." Going to church makes them look good, at least on the outside. So it gets them what they want. Let's chase that!

Or maybe they replace Jesus with "being a good person." Helping others makes them feel good, and it helps them gain friends. It gets them what they want.

And in the process, Jesus gets left behind.

See, many people think they're chasing Jesus when really they're chasing all that other stuff: happiness or wealth or acceptance. Instead of reading the Bible and seeing who Jesus really is and how he truly saved them, they chase after temporary saviors.

Which brings us back to you. Is Jesus your MacGuffin? Is he replaceable to you? Only a tool to get your story moving, to get you what you really want?

Fake Jesuses can be easily replaced. But the real Jesus? Acts 4:12 says, "There is salvation in no one else, for there is no other name under heaven given to people by which we must be saved." He is utterly irreplaceable. He disagrees with you all the time. He calls you out on your sin. He is an untamed man who is never what you think he is. And he loves you and forgives you and accepts you.

How can you tell if your Jesus is the real Jesus? Be in your Bible. When the Bible says something you disagree with, trust that God knew what he was doing when he had the Bible written. He knows more than you.

And see that Jesus himself is worth chasing. He is the treasure that we need.

Psalm 73:25: "Who do I have in heaven but you? And I desire nothing on earth but you."

Prayer: Jesus, forgive me when I use you as a MacGuffin to chase after something else. Help me to see the real you. Make me hunger for who you really are, and help me to rejoice in you. Amen.

Fake Jesuses can be easily replaced. But the real Jesus? He is utterly unreplaceable.

The Me MacGuffin

Are you a MacGuffin for Jesus? You've heard before, in this book, that he paid for you. I've told you again and again that he died on a cross, paying in blood to make you his own.

But are you just a MacGuffin?

If we replaced you with, say, Sir Not-Appearing-In-This-Book, would Jesus have done the same thing? Would it change anything in the "plot" of our world, the plot of Jesus becoming human to save sinners?

Well, the Bible's clear that God loves the entire world. Heaven is filled with people from every tribe, every nation, every language. God doesn't want anyone to die, but for everyone to come to a knowledge of the truth (1 Timothy 2:4). So, yes, Jesus would have died for Sir Not-Appearing-In-This-Book, too. He wouldn't hesitate.

But you are no MacGuffin because he died for *you*. He has prepared a place in heaven for you. Yes, he did the same for the person who lives a few minutes from your house and for the person on the other side of the world.

But he also did it for you.

Listen to what the Bible says in 1 Peter 2:9-10: "But you are a chosen race, a royal priesthood, a holy nation, a people for his possession, so that you may proclaim the praises of the one who called you out of darkness into his marvelous light. Once you were not a people, but now you are God's people; you had not received mercy, but now you have received mercy."

You see that?

Chosen.

Jesus looks at you and grins. No, you could never be replaced. You are his own special, chosen person.

Definitely not a MacGuffin.

Prayer: Jesus, thank you for choosing me and making me your own. Help me to rejoice every day that you have made me your very own. Amen.

Trope Twelve

The Heroic Sacrifice

AS ALWAYS, SIR WAIST-NOT SAVES
HIS FRIENDS FROM THE SNACK TABLE OF TERROR.

Trope 12: The Heroic Sacrifice

The City of Mirrors and Moonlight

Only a few more minutes.

Mirrored skyscrapers surrounded the square. A fountain gurgled in the center. In a few hours, cars would be honking as they tried to make their way through downtown, but now everything was silent, except for the sound of two men battling for the fate of the city.

Valdren wrapped his fingers around Drake's throat. "You thought you could usurp me?" he hissed. His fangs glistened in the moonlight. "I built this city. I made sure everyone would feel safe here. Mirrored buildings, so no one can sneak up on you."

"No one, except a vampire," Drake croaked.

Valdren grinned. "And so I am free to hunt a people so very confident in themselves." He squeezed a little harder. Pain lanced through Drake's body. "You thought you could free them. But no one can stand up to me."

Drake gurgled and pointed to the hand around his throat.

"You wish to speak your final words?"

He nodded.

Valdren lessened his grip. "I will allow you that much."

Drake sucked in a huge breath. "Yeah, see, you can't kill me by cutting off airflow. I just need it to talk."

The ancient vampire narrowed his eyes. "What?"

"Take a look in the mirror."

Valdren's eyes shot to the skyscraper across the plaza, to its mirrored surface. He couldn't see himself.

And he couldn't see Drake.

"Oops. I guess I never told you, huh?" He kicked back against Valdren, flipping around and landing in a crouch. "I'm a lot harder to kill than most of the people who've stood up against you."

The elder vampire hissed and flew toward Drake. There was no way the younger man could dodge. Valdren was just too strong. He didn't stand a chance.

He just needed another minute.

The dark lord of the mirrored city struck Drake. He felt the bones in his neck crack. He fell to the pavement, unable to move.

"Oh, I will savor this," Valdren said as he stooped to pick Drake up by the throat. "You're not clever enough by half, boy."

"Oh, clever enough," he whispered. "See, I knew you'd come out to get me. But it's dawn."

"I stand in shadows. I'm safe."

"Mirrors don't reflect vampires, but they do reflect sunlight."

The sun burst over the horizon to the east. The great mirrors of the skyscrapers reflected golden light through the city streets.

Valdren burst into flames. He snarled, "You'll die, too."

"Worth it," Drake said as his hair burned. "The city's safe now. No vampires at all."

A Sacrificial Trope

When evil threatens, heroes must rise. They stand against the onslaught. Ah, but there is a cost for good to triumph. A sacrifice must be made.

> *Heroes will go to any length, even sacrificing their lives, to protect the world and fight evil.*

Is it Ben Kenobi letting himself die so Luke Skywalker can escape? Is it Boromir staying behind to make sure the hobbits are safe? Is it Spock sacrificing himself for the *Enterprise*? Or is it Iron Man snapping his fingers to save the world? (Sorry, spoilers!)

Heroes will go to any length, even sacrificing their lives, to protect the world and fight evil.

This is the heroic sacrifice.

Whatever the Cost

How far will a hero go to save his people? In many stories, there's a cost. Sometimes it's the cost of losing a relationship or being thought to be powerless. That version of the trope often plays out in superhero stories. Spider-Man gives up his relationship to Mary Jane. Barry Allen is always late, even though he's the Flash. It's not just in superhero stories, though. Captain Janeway destroys the only way home for her ship and crew at the end of *Star Trek: Voyager*'s first episode to protect countless lives.

But often enough, it costs so much more. The music swells. The main character realizes what must be done. He stands tall.

And he dies.

The Harry Potter series is full of these kinds of sacrifices. Ron is willing to die so Harry can get to the Sorcerer's Stone. Dumbledore allows himself to be killed. Even Harry walks toward certain death so his friends can live in the final book.

Maybe one of these or another heroic sacrifice actually caused you tears. I know I get a little choked up if the story is strong enough. And there's a reason: You're seeing a reflection of Jesus.

Sacrifice

Cultures have long understood the idea of sacrifice. One person or thing must die in the place of another, as a substitute. God actually made use of that reflection for centuries before Jesus's arrival, pointing to the truth: Someone must pay the cost of sin. All

> *One person or thing must die in the place of another, as a substitute.*

through the Old Testament of the Bible, before Jesus came, God's people offered sacrifices. They killed countless lambs. Animals died to pay for their sins every day. All the blood of beasts didn't forgive anything, though (Hebrews 9:9). They just pointed ahead to the sacrifice Jesus would make.

And Jesus did sacrifice himself. He realized what had to be done to protect his people. He willingly paid the cost: his own life.

And his sacrifice worked. Sin doesn't chain you anymore. Death itself is defeated; Jesus rose from the dead and crushed it. You are free!

> **But when Jesus sacrificed himself, it was enough.**

So, appreciate the reflection of the heroic sacrifice when you see or read it. Use that to point to the greater sacrifice Jesus made and appreciate that real event even more.

But there is something to watch out for. Just because someone sacrifices himself, that doesn't mean it's an effective sacrifice. Ben Kenobi sacrificed himself in *Star Wars*, but what did that accomplish? Luke Skywalker escaped, sure, but he still had to come back to blow up the Death Star! His sacrifice didn't save everyone, except maybe indirectly! Boromir fought to save the hobbits, but they were still captured by the enemy. And superheroes? When they sacrifice themselves, there are *always* more supervillains!

Perhaps the closest we get is the great illustration of Jesus's sacrifice from *The Lion, the Witch, and the Wardrobe*. Now, C. S. Lewis, the author, wrote that book as a direct picture of Jesus's sacrifice. So yes, you really should see a reflection of Jesus there! Aslan trades his life to free the traitor Edmund. He allows himself to die. And then he comes back to life. That reflects the truth of Jesus's sacrifice for us. But even in that story, there is still a great battle to be fought against the White Witch. The work isn't done.

But when Jesus sacrificed himself, it was enough. No enemy remained. No other work needed to be done. In fact, that was his cry from the cross: "It is finished!" (John 19:30).

So, what made Jesus an acceptable sacrifice? How could he get it all done with one death?

Jesus was a perfect substitute because he was one of us! He was human. But he wasn't *just* human. He was even better. He was sinless, meaning his sacrifice could count for everyone. He was God, able to pay any price and have it count.

But here's the biggest difference between Jesus and just about every other example of heroic sacrifice (except maybe that Aslan one): Jesus returned from the dead because death couldn't wrap its fingers around him. He was perfect, so he never deserved death. He conquered even that enemy. And unlike C. S. Lewis's story, or any other story, that was the end. No enemies remained. Jesus conquered them all. For us.

Now that's an awesome sacrifice and worthy of the swelling music of a great soundtrack. But the fact that he lives now? That's even better.

How Far Do I Have to Go?

So, Jesus sacrificed himself. And we love stories where the hero lays down his life.

Does that mean I need to sacrifice myself? Is it good for me to sacrifice myself?

Yes!

And no.

The Bible does say that no one has greater love than the person who lays down his life for his friends (John 15:13). But let's face it: There aren't a lot of opportunities to do that. I've never (knowingly) faced a supervillain, and orcs don't seem to wander the area I live in. There aren't even Sith Lords for me to stand up against!

Notice that the focus of that verse isn't about laying down your life, but about love.

But notice that the focus of that verse isn't about laying down your life, but about love. The greatest evidence of love is laying down your life. And who loved that much? Jesus.

Now you're called to love. And oftentimes love doesn't mean sacrificing your life—or, at least, it doesn't mean you have to die. See, it can mean sacrificing your time or your energy for another person. And that often takes even more courage because you're not usually noticed for that. No one's building huge statues for the woman who sacrifices her time to take care of her little sister or pick up a little bit of litter.

But that's sacrifice, too!

One of my favorite shows is *Babylon 5*. At one point Captain Sheridan makes a huge sacrifice to stop the Shadows, and he lies dying. Lorien, an ancient being, offers the captain a choice: "It's easy to find something worth dying for. Do you have anything worth living for?"

So, are you called to make a heroic sacrifice?

Yes. Yes, you are.

Can you imagine a story where the great sacrifice, the cost, is that the hero must turn away from battle and go home to take care of the kids? Talk about anticlimactic! And yet, so often, that is a better sacrifice. It shows an immense amount of love to put in that time and effort to love your family, your friends, your congregation.

So, are you called to make a heroic sacrifice?

Yes. Yes, you are. But that doesn't mean you're called to die. You're called to lay down your life in service to others, to love others, because Jesus first loved you (1 John 4:19).

Using Heroic Sacrifices to Share Jesus

You ever notice how many main characters have to sacrifice their lives at the end of the story? Why do you think that is?

Most of the time, those heroes are awesome. But I know someone whose sacrifice was even better. Let me tell you about Jesus…

Are You Pondering What I'm Pondering?

The next time you encounter a story that has a heroic sacrifice, ask yourself these questions:

- ✓ Why did the hero have to sacrifice himself or herself?
- ✓ What did the sacrifice accomplish? What did it leave undone?
- ✓ Was the benefit worth the cost of that sacrifice?

The next time you enjoy a story that has a heroic sacrifice, ask yourself these questions:

- ✓ What emotional reaction do you have to the sacrifice?
- ✓ In what ways does this sacrifice reflect Jesus's sacrifice for you?
- ✓ Were there other sacrifices the hero made before the "big sacrifice" that moved you as much? Why or why not?

Meditations on Heroic Sacrifices

What Do You Give Up?

When I do marriage counseling, I'll ask the husband if he's willing to give up his life for his wife. The answer invariably is, "Of course!" He's thinking of a dramatic scene where a guy pulls a gun on them and he steps between his wife and danger. He'd take a bullet for her, and he'd be a hero!

Then I'll ask, "Are you willing to give up the TV remote for her?"

And he'll look really, really uncomfortable.

> *Servants don't usually go out in a blaze of glory. Usually they, you know, serve.*

How about you? Would you be willing to give up your life for someone else, but not willing to give up your phone? Would you take a bullet, but not take out the trash?

Why is that?

We all want to be someone else's hero. If we go out in a blaze of glory, we know others will talk about it. We'll have rescued another person and gotten a huge, dramatic moment.

But to do the dishes? To mow the lawn? Where's the drama? Where's the heroism?

What did Jesus say? "Whoever wants to become great among you will be your servant, and whoever wants to be first among you will be a slave to all. For even the Son of Man did not come to be served, but to serve, and to give his life as a ransom for many" (Mark 10:43-45). Servants don't usually go out in a blaze of glory. Usually they, you know, serve.

But when Jesus returns, he won't say, "If you gave your life for another person, I'll welcome you to heaven!" When he describes what someone who trusts in him looks like, he talks about things like giving water to someone who's thirsty or visiting someone who's alone (Matthew 25:31-46).

That might sound disappointing to you, but it's a huge encouragement. When Jesus looks at your life, he doesn't just look at the big dramatic moments. He sees those little acts that are invisible to everyone else. He sees what you've done out of love for another. He sees what you've given up: the hours, the energy, the opportunities. And those sacrifices are not forgotten.

And those opportunities you've rejected? Those sacrifices you said were too much, like taking out the garbage? Yep. Those are sins.

But Jesus didn't just sacrifice his life for you. He gave every moment of every day for you. And when Jesus died, he didn't die just for the things you've done, but for all the sacrifices you didn't make, too. He chose to sacrifice himself even for people like us. And by his sacrifice, we are forgiven.

Prayer: Jesus, you sacrificed yourself for me, your entire life. Guide me to love you and sacrifice everything I am to you, every day of my life. Amen.

It's Not Enough

"No one has greater love than this: to lay down his life for his friends" (John 15:13).

That means that every single person who's ever laid down his life for someone else gets to go to heaven, right?

That's… that's not what the Bible says. Here's an uncomfortable truth: One great act of love does not negate even a single sin. Think about this.

Pretend that there's a person who is upright. He's done so much good for his community. He knows so many people personally and has improved the lives of everyone he knows. Well, everyone except that one young woman. See, she's paralyzed for life now. One night that man was drunk and got behind the wheel of his car and hit her.

Would you tell that woman that the man shouldn't be punished because of all the good things he's done? I really, really hope you wouldn't. That man has sinned in a terrible way and deserves punishment. And if that's true of a person who does one evil thing after a lifetime of good, why would one great act of love negate a lifetime of sins, or any sins in the life of someone else?

Jesus never said, "For God so loved the world, that whoever lays down his life for his friends will not die but have eternal life." He said something very, very different. "For God loved the world in this way: He gave his one and only Son, so that everyone who believes in him will not perish but have eternal life" (John 3:16).

The only thing that saves us is Jesus's sacrifice on the cross.

No one gets into heaven because they laid down their life for someone else. That action requires great love, and I'll still give such a great sacrifice great respect, but we can't earn our way into heaven by what we do, even by sacrificing our life to save another.

The only thing that saves us is Jesus's sacrifice on the cross.

And that means that yes, we can still get choked up when we hear about real-life examples of someone sacrificing themselves to save another. But let's not say more than what the Bible says.

If anyone gets into heaven, it's all Jesus's doing, not ours. I'm not going to trust what I do, no matter how big and heroic it might be. I'd rather trust the God that saved me by laying his life down for me. I could never do enough. But he is all I need. His sacrifice is enough.

Prayer: Jesus, you saved me. Help me to trust you and not my actions, no matter how heroic they may be. Instead, help me to love you first and to love the people around me with all my actions. Amen.

Not Dramatic Enough

River Song sacrifices herself so the Doctor can live. Spock dies to save his friend. Superman perishes to stop Doomsday.

And I don't know about you, but I get a little weepy. I mean, the music swells, and these characters I've learned to love are dead or dying. You've gone a journey with them, and now it's all at an end, a beautiful sacrifice to save others.

But then you read about Jesus dying on the cross, and maybe you feel something, but my guess is you don't get as weepy. Or if you do, it's not very often. Why not? Isn't Jesus worth shedding a few tears?

Well, I want to comfort you first of all: Jesus never says, "Thou shalt get weepy over me." Emotional reactions can be a good thing, but Jesus never commands them. We really need to be careful that our emotions are reactions to reality and not let our emotions determine reality! If you don't get weepy over Jesus's death, don't worry. I'm not saying that you're sinning by not bursting into tears!

I am presenting a comparison, though. Why might we get emotional over books and movies but not over Jesus? After all, the books and movies are fiction. We know they're fake. I'm sorry to break it to you, but *The Lord of the Rings* isn't a documentary, and *Star Wars* really didn't happen a long time ago. Jesus, on the other hand, really lived, died, and rose again.

So, what's going on?

I think part of it is familiarity. Especially if you regularly attend the same congregation, you may hear the same truth expressed the same way. It's hard to get emotional over something that you can speak by rote. (That said, I do know some people who can quote most of *The Princess Bride* and still get emotional. So knowing something by rote doesn't negate emotion!)

But a huge part of it is our sinful nature. We all have these sinful natures that don't want us to celebrate Jesus. If that wicked part of us can convince us that Jesus is boring, it's much closer to winning.

So, what do we do?

First, know who you are. You are not your sinful nature. You *are* a Christian. You *have* a sinful nature.

Second, take time in confession. If you're not sure of your sins, walk through the Ten Commandments, and really dig into what they mean. As you confess your sins, see that Jesus loves you and has forgiven all of them. You may be amazed at how emotional confession and the announcement of forgiveness can be!

Third, take time on your own to see with wonder what Jesus has done for you. That may mean reading a book that digs further into Jesus's heroic sacrifice. (I personally recommend *A Violent Grace* by Michael Card.) That may mean reading the original in the Bible, too! Check out Luke 22-24, for instance.

Fourth, when you see those heroic sacrifices and you get emotional, pause and thank God that Jesus's sacrifice is far greater. "Otherwise, he would have had to suffer many times since the foundation of the world. But now he has appeared one time, at the end of the ages, for the removal of sin by the sacrifice of himself" (Hebrews 9:26).

Prayer: Lord, help me to marvel at your sacrifice. Direct my emotions to reflect reality and let me be amazed that you would die for a sinner like me. Amen.

You are not your sinful nature. You are a Christian. You have a sinful nature.

Post-Credits Scene

Why Tropes Matter

Post-Credits Scene: Why Tropes Matter

Deleted Scenes

Chanomax brought his fingers into the silent repose position, readying the incantation. His arms shook. His throat burned.

Balor chuckled. "I've stolen your voice, wizard. And without that you're useless. A wizard without magic is nothing!"

Chanomax smiled. There was more than one way to use language, more than one way to "speak" an incantation. He signed the runes.

The spell exploded from the air in front of him, racing toward Balor, enveloping him in…

> *"Sorry. The author decided to not use your chapter."*

Something tore through reality. A young woman with short blond hair stuck her head through the tear. "Hey, Channy? Sorry. The author decided to not use your chapter."

"What?" The wizard looked around at his now-frozen world. "How can you write a book about geeky things and not talk about magic?"

"The same way you don't talk about superpowers, I guess." She shrugged. "Want to come to the break room?"

"Well, if I won't have my epic battle with my nemesis, may as well," he grumbled. He climbed into the tear in reality and glanced around, spotting a group of scruffy people in long brown coats. "Wait a second. He didn't talk about plucky rebels either?"

"Something about running out of room in the book."

"Well, I feel useless."

"Tell me about it."

A Trope Unaddressed

But what about magic? What about superpowers? What about barbarians and starship captains that love their ships and plucky rebels? What about all those other tropes?

There really are a lot of tropes, aren't there? Fantasy and science fiction have so many. Weapons that can destroy worlds. Magic swords. Alien conquerors. Traitors. We could go on and on, couldn't we?

But, alas, every book must end, and we have come to the end of this one.

This last little chapter is about all the other tropes we haven't touched on yet.

Sometimes You Just Gotta Figure It Out Yourself

So, what should you do when you run into all those other tropes? Because, let's face it, most stories you encounter will probably use tropes that we never touched on here.

Use your discernment.

It really is that simple and that impossible.

Use your discernment.

It really is that simple and that impossible.

Throughout this book, you've been introduced to questions to use when you encounter individual tropes. Hopefully, you can use those questions as a model of questions to ask about any trope. I'm hoping you're equipped now! Start thinking that way about anything you encounter:

What is the problem?

What is the proposed solution?

Why am I enjoying this?

And take your answers to the Bible. Compare what you find with what the Bible says. And that means... well, you need geek out about God's Word as much as you geek out about, say, *Star Trek* or *The Lord of the Rings* or any other geeky pursuit.

And that may be the most challenging thing of all.

Because let's face it: Most of the time it's easier to geek out about a favorite book series or TV show or movie.

You know why that is? There are two big reasons:

> The Bible wasn't written to entertain. It was written so that you could get to know Jesus.

The Bible wasn't written to entertain. It was written so that you could get to know Jesus. As *The Jesus Storybook Bible* says, "Every story whispers his name." Every page in the Bible points to our sin and our need for a Savior... and the fact that our Savior did come.

But compare that to, say, *Star Trek*. It is written primarily to entertain. Which means, to put it bluntly, it's easier to gulp down without having to think, usually. *Star Trek* includes cliffhangers and special effects. The Bible doesn't have too many cliffhangers.

And that gets us to the second reason why it's hard to geek out over the Bible: We have sinful natures that really don't want us geeking out over what Jesus has done. Those sinful natures hate Jesus and will do whatever it takes to keep us away. But geeking out over *Game of Thrones* or *Doctor Who*? The sinful nature generally won't fight against that!

So why is it hard to geek out over Jesus? Because he's not designed to entertain, and you've got your sinful nature fighting against you.

What are you going to do about it?

Geeking Out Over God

Some people are foodies. They love watching shows about food. They'll subscribe to YouTube channels where people tour restaurants. They'll have pretentious ingredients. They geek out over food.

Maybe you're not a foodie. Maybe you just say, "Get me a hamburger. Whatever." You tend to not geek out over food.

But this unites the two: They both need food to live.

Whether or not you're a foodie, you'll eat. Maybe you'll even put in the effort to eat relatively healthy meals. You know that if you don't eat, there's gonna be some problems on the horizon.

In the same way, you might never geek out over God's Word. You might not go, "Oh, cool!" over the book of Numbers or the way that Jesus's genealogy is amazing. Whether or not you ever geek out over the Bible, though, you still need it to live.

Now, whether someone is a foodie or not, I know that pretty much anyone with working taste buds loves certain foods. Maybe for you it's tacos or burgers or filet mignon, but there's certain foods that you do get excited about.

In the same way, I hope you get excited about certain parts of Scripture. Maybe it's not the book of Numbers. Maybe you love the stories from the book of Judges. Maybe you're drawn to the teachings in 1 Corinthians. And if you've never geeked out over any part of the Bible, it may be that you're not familiar with those sections that best match your personality. The Bible is full of a whole bunch of different kinds of literature, because God knew that he created us to be a bunch of different kinds of people.

But, again, if you're reading the Bible well, you'll see that every story whispers Jesus's name.

And ultimately, he is worth geeking out over.

Is there any hero that has ever faced more daunting odds?

Is there any protagonist who has ever defeated a more dangerous enemy?

Is there any character that has ever shown greater love?

You see, Jesus is worth geeking out over. Unlike any of the fiction we've talked about here, Jesus is real. And he fought for you. He rescued you from your sin, from your guilt.

So, yeah, the Bible wasn't written to entertain, but it has a lot to do with you. And your sinful nature doesn't want you to geek out over it; maybe that's a sign that you really should dig in deeper.

And the more you dig into the Bible, the more you will see reflections of what it says about the world in the various geeky stories you enjoy. You'll be able to make connections you never did before. You'll be more equipped to use discernment as you encounter more tropes.

A Final Farewell

I hope the book has helped you, and maybe even entertained you. I hope it's helped you grow in your appreciation of some geeky stuff we have.

But even more, I hope it's helped you grow closer to Jesus.

Go. Be geeks.

But even more, be godly.

> *The more you dig into the Bible, the more you will see reflections of what it says about the world in the geeky stories you enjoy.*

"Made it!"

CPSIA information can be obtained
at www.ICGtesting.com
Printed in the USA
JSHW050050270521
15231JS00006B/109